America's Elite Colleges

Colleges

The Smart Applicant's Guide to the Ivy League
and Other Top schools

America's Elite Colleges

The Smart Applicant's Guide
to the Ivy League
and Other Top Schools

by Dave Berry and David Hawsey

Random House, Inc.
New York
www.review.com

Princeton Review Publishing, L. L. C.
2315 Broadway
New York, NY 10024
E-mail: comments@review.com

ISBN 0-375-76206-X

Editor: Erik Olson
Designer: Greta Englert
Production Editor: Kristen Azzara
Production Coordinator: Greta Englert

Manufactured in the United States of America.

9 8 7 6 5 4 3 2 1

Acknowledgements

From Dave Berry

Writing a book is a birthing process, complete with a gestation period (this one's conception occurred in 1994), much nurturing, and labor pains. Delivery, however, requires the help of others. Thanks to the following people who were part of bringing this simple volume to life.

My family: Sharon, wife, friend, and helper, overflowing with faith, support, patience, and love; Leigh Ann and John, daughter and son, my pride and joy, this father's greatest treasure; and Else and Greta, miniature Dachshunds, my constant, affectionate companions.

My co-author: David Hawsey, man of vision and perfect complement, who believed in this idea from the start and partnered magnificently, like the gentleman and professional he is.

My personal friends: Gary Reid and his brother, Mike, lifelong confidants and sanity anchors, who kept me laughing; Frank "The Coach" Fedeli, my mentor, who taught me the importance of book layout and greater love of family; and Farran Zerbe, fellow classical music lover, who always told me I could write, and I believed him.

My work friends at The Hancock Group, Inc. (THG): Allan Hancock, who gives me the forum and freedom to be creative;

THG's executive board, who underwrite me; Joe Cavrich, whose sage legal advice I honor; and my fellow workers, who understand me (I think).

The Princeton Review: John Katzman and Evan Schnittman, for believing that our book should be read; Robert Franek, who mixes mature business savvy with endless good cheer; and Erik Olson, our editor, whose youthful talent and objective perspectives made this book better.

Random House: Jeanne Krier, publicist supreme, wry wit, and Ivy parent, for kindness beyond the call; and Tom Russell, marketing guru, whose support behind the scenes made many good things happen about which we were unaware.

Finally, Judith Schnell, publishing maven, who unselfishly shared her considerable industry knowledge with me; and, certainly not least of all, the very talented students who gave me permission to quote them and use their superb essays: Julie Chow, Jeff Fine, and Monica Candal.

From David Hawsey

In memory of Gladys K. Hawsey (Mom), and dedicated to Walter W. Hawsey, Jr. (Dad)—To new beginnings! We love you, and are always here to support you.

To Joan, Sarah, Daniel, Nathan and Maggie—For your patience, support and love: I am an empty shell of a man without you in my life!

To fellow "shellback" and co-author Dave Berry—For your extraordinary advocacy of student achievement, and for your unselfish encouragement during our ongoing quest.

The Staff of Princeton Review: Erik Olson, you have a real gift. Thanks for being our guide.

Dr. Thomas Canavan—My former professor and dean at Drexel University, and currently provost at Providence College (RI)—for teaching me how to write well.

George Dolnikowski—Professor emeritus, Harvard graduate, gentle spirit and "Prekrasnaya Dusha."

Robert W. "Big Daddy" Neff—Yale alumnus, retired college president, friend, humanitarian and mentor: Thank you for investing in my family, time and time again. You are the very definition of servant leadership.

Dr. Peter T. Mitchell, President of Albion College. You are a visionary leader of an exceptional college, and model "Liberal Arts At Work" better than anyone I have ever met. It is an honor to serve you. *Lux Fiat!*

Donald D. Moyer—Graduate of Bryn Mawr and Muhlenberg College, world-class expert in sustainable economic development, friend and fishing buddy, and unquestionably the greatest mentor I could have ever hoped for. You put the joy and spirit back into my career, helped transform my life, and taught me to "savor the pause" along the journey. This is one "big fish" that didn't get away!

And to all students who are just beginning the college search: The college you attend doesn't characterize who you are. It's the value you place on your family and friends. We simply give you the tools— now go use them!

Contents

Foreword

We buy up magazines and books that lead us to the best of everything—be it hamburgers, bargains, restaurants, doctors, SAT prep courses, or colleges. It's fun to see what someone else deems the best and to ask what criteria he used to determine that status. What makes a bagel "the best" bagel? When we sample it, do we agree? *America's Elite Colleges* selects thirty-two colleges as the nation's most outstanding. Among the country's nearly 3,000 four-year colleges, about 225 are thought to have "highly selective" admission policies. The thirty-two elite colleges are beyond "highly selective." Most of their admitted students were in the top 10% of their high school classes. To be competitive in these elite applicant pools, you must be exceptional—the academic and personal equivalent of an Olympic gold medallist. If your profile fits this description, you can use this book to help you understand what these colleges are looking for and how to pitch your application effectively. If you are reading it as a ninth- or tenth-grader, it can serve as a training manual to get you buff; fit to be a gold-medal contender by your senior year.

Over the past three years, increasing numbers of high school graduates have led to record numbers of college applications and, consequently, lower acceptance rates at almost all colleges. Counselors have had to redefine which are "safe" colleges and consider the strategic advantages of advising students to apply

Early Decision to colleges, which, intent on shaking images as fallbacks to the Ivies, have filled nearly half of their freshman classes by Early Decision. Three colleges among the thirty-two profiled in this book—Harvard, Columbia, and Brown—reported all-time low acceptance rates last year of 10.9%, 14.9%, and 15.1%, respectively. About 16% of applicants to Harvard placed first in their graduating classes. Those three colleges no doubt could put together a second, equally strong freshman class by selecting from among those students whom they denied admission.

These facts are meant to be informative, not discouraging. Every year bright, qualified students are indeed admitted to elite colleges. You want to be one of them. Applying to any of these colleges is hard work. As you will read in the introduction to this book, "the winners...have to somehow stand out from the rest of the best." *America's Elite Colleges* is filled with real-life examples, strategic application tips, and explanations of concepts such as enrollment management and temperament to show you how to present yourself as a distinct individual who will be chosen to contribute to that well-rounded freshman class.

The first part of the book provides a highly informative roadmap to guide you through the blind turns and roadblocks of the application process. "Process" is a key word. Admission to an elite college, or to any college for that matter, is not only about "getting there;" it is as much about the journey that takes you there. This book puts you, the applicant, in the driver's seat and shows you how to navigate. Elite colleges are impressed by students who take the wheel and show that they are in charge of their part of the process and of their lives. It shows you how to stand out, to jump off the page at midnight when the admission officer reading your application is on her tenth cup of coffee and hundredth essay of the day. Success in the college application process depends upon thoughtful planning, not on dumb luck, especially if your targets are the elite colleges. The students whom they admit have taken learning seriously, reached out beyond themselves to the community, and demonstrated leadership, talent, and a strong sense of self. Your essays will show you reflecting on some of these overall experiences and explaining how they have helped shape you.

As you read through the profiles of these thirty-two most selective colleges, I urge you to look past their prestigious reputations to the specific characteristics that define each of them and do or do not make them a good match for you. Each has a distinct personality, much like your own temperament snapshot. Would you rather be able to head out for a quick run on the slopes in the mountains or order Chinese food at midnight in the big city? Do you want an active Greek life on campus; stringent core curriculum requirements, or more open choices; small seminar classes that meet around a table, or large lectures taught by teaching assistants? Chapters four through six provide tips and guidelines to help you determine a match, urging you to think for yourself as you evaluate your credentials and qualifications and set them against a college's resources and atmosphere.

If you gain entry into one of these colleges, you'll discover that those attributes that have rendered them "elite" stem from the importance they place within their educational communities on merit; social, economic, and racial diversity; talent and creativity; intellectual curiosity; cultural and global awareness; and respect for the individual voice. "Elite" applies only to the selective level of admission, not to any stereotypical preconception about privilege or entitlement.

The Story of You that you tell throughout your application, from the courses you have selected, to your lofty test scores and grades, to your essays and interviews, should be just that—YOUR story and no one else's. It is very important that your individual voice be heard. You need to show how you will use and add to the resources and community of each college. *America's Elite Colleges* shows you how, and also profiles the stats and environments of the thirty-two elite colleges. As you read it, ask yourself if you and these colleges are a match, or if, by taking the advice in this book, you have time to become one.

Frank C. Leana, Ph.D.
Educational Counselor
New York City &
Cambridge, Massachusetts

Introduction

Who Should Read This Book

This book is for high school students, their parents, and even those students and parents who have years to go before they have to face choosing, applying to, and attending college. Regardless of how much you've read about elite college admissions, you'll find valuable help in these pages.

What This Book Can Do for You

Thanks to its many real-life examples you'll see the level at which successful elite college applicants perform. We'll equip you with an arsenal of strategic tips for use in your applications, regardless of what colleges are on your wish list. You're going to find out how to gather, analyze, and correlate information about who you are and craft your application into the story of you. We'll have some fun along the way, too, showing you how to blend some humor into your application, which goes a long way with an admissions committee. We think you'll find our approach holistic. That is, the total effect of our method will be far greater than the sum of the book's individual chapters.

Preparation Is the Key

Putting together a successful application to an elite college is like painting a car. In your mind, you can see the finished product gleaming and looking spectacular, the envy of your friends. Before you apply that first coat of paint, though, you have to go through a rigorous preparation process—scraping, sanding, filling in rough spots, and taping off those things that won't get painted. Prepping is about 80% of the work.

With applications, your job is to find out as much as possible about yourself and your dream colleges. This means research, and a lot of it. Then you've got to show the admissions committee that you and their college are a perfect match. And if you've researched your reasons for your compatibility, the application might write itself.

We're not going to show you ultra-competitive college admissions through rose-colored lenses. But if you're qualified, we encourage you to think as if you're the number-one Ivy applicant that every college will want as a first-round draft pick. Start with an attitude of success, rather than an attitude of I-probably-won't-make-it-but-I-guess-I'll-apply-anyway.

Don't think that this is a weekend job. It's going to require a lot of work from you. It's doable, though. After all, thousands of students have gotten into the nation's best schools for years. When you finish reading this book, you'll know how they did it.

Part I

The Challenge

Chapter 1

Class of '04:
Toughest Ticket Yet

Adjust Your Thinking

You've picked up this book looking for the Ultimate Truth about getting into the most elite colleges in America, right? And what is it? Well, the truth is, there is no truth or formula. The rules change as quickly as do the criteria for selecting this year's number-one college in the *U.S. News* rankings. We know two things for sure about these toughest-to-get-into colleges, though:

1. The elite colleges are getting harder to get into every year. They search for good applicants, but reject great students through seemingly arbitrary decisions.

2. The admission process was designed to meet colleges' need to build great classes, not for your educational or emotional benefit.

It's a Steep Slope Out There

Think about the acceptance rates of the most selective national colleges and universities. The percentages come from dividing the total number of admission letters sent out by the total number of applications received. For example, Amherst College received 5,351 applications and admitted 1,035 for an acceptance rate of 19%. Are you freaked out? Amherst's acceptance rate isn't the lowest in the land! Check out these rates from the twenty-one hardest-to-get-into colleges.

Amherst College	19%
Brown University	16%
Columbia University	14%
Cooper Union	13%
Dartmouth College	21%
Duke University	26%
Georgetown University	22%

Harvard University	11%
Massachusetts Institute of Technology	19%
Northwestern University	32%
Princeton University	12%
Stanford University	13%
Swarthmore College	22%
United States Air Force Academy	18%
United States Military Academy	13%
United States Naval Academy	15%
University of Notre Dame	34%
University of Pennsylvania	23%
Williams College	24%
Yale University	16%

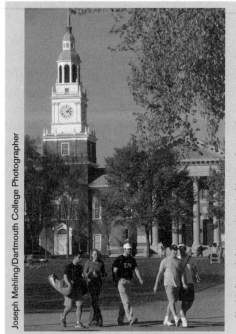

Joseph Mehling/Dartmouth College Photographer

With just over 4,000 undergraduates, Dartmouth College is the smallest Ivy League school. Dartmouth's web site notes that a third of its Class of 2004 were captains of a high school sports teams, a third were either valedictorians or salutatorians, and over 86% ranked in the top 10% of their graduating classes. An impressive 75% scored above 1350 on the SAT. Dartmouth graduates rank second only to Princeton's in their annual-giving participation, a key indicator of overall student satisfaction.

So How Do They Choose?

Ethan Bronner, in an excellent *New York Times* article on admissions to these schools, quotes Dartmouth's Dean of Admissions, Karl Furstenberg, on the subject of the large number of qualified applicants to his school. Furstenberg said that the large number of strong candidates "makes our job harder, but it forces us to look at the intangibles ...."[1]

Last year was the toughest admissions year ever. Many seniors with 1550+ SAT Is and 770+ SAT IIs (etc., etc.) were either rejected or waitlisted. Academic and test score superiority are a good start, but they won't kick open the doors to these schools. Where can you get an edge? The key lies in Dean Furstenberg's intangibles.

Finding the Musicians

Every four years, the Van Cliburn International Piano Competition takes place in Ft. Worth, Texas. In it the young pianists from around the globe compete for the world's top prizes in their art. This competition is very much like the elite college admission process.

The sheer number of entrants with awesome talent would make your head spin. In fact, so many terrific pianists want to compete in the Cliburn that the judges travel to other countries to audition them for a chance to become applicants. In other words, the pianists have to apply just to compete.

Like these ultra-skilled pianists, just about every student applying to the most selective schools in America has virtuoso numbers. And with so many kids with the scores, grades, and extracurriculars of prodigies means that the winners—the admitted students—have to somehow stand out from the rest of the best. One of the judges

---

[1] Ethan Bronner, "For '99 College Applicants, Stiffest Competition Ever." *New York Times*, June 12, 1999.

of the Cliburn told us that a pianist merely "playing all the notes correctly" didn't earn his vote. The true musicians, the kids whose playing touched him on an internal level, were the ones that walked away with a victory. And that's what you're going to have to do: Make the admissions committee respect your academic accomplishments and then stand out (in a good way) by showing that you're an inspired, passionate person.

Are You a Contender?

There are some raw numbers that you'll need before you're even considered a player in this process. Your test scores, class rank, and grade point average (GPA) should look something like the ones in the profiles in the back of this book.

Don't panic if you don't measure up on every indicator. The average scores of the middle 50% of admitted students are just that: the average of the middle. Many applicants came in below each of those averages. If you're behind on every indicator, though, and you're not an Olympic athlete, you should understand that the odds are stacked against you.

How Do You Begin?

You already have. Now read the rest of this book.

If we've done our job, you'll learn to realistically assess your chances, focus your energy, and put together a stellar application. What's better, you'll understand your temperament, interests, and why you'll love college.

Chapter 2

Enrollment Management:
What You Think About It

Wouldn't it be great if you could know exactly what criteria your top-choice college or university uses to accept students and to know all the inside tips before you start your applications? Wouldn't it be equally useful to know specifically how your family's financial information is used when the schools are determining scholarships and grants for you?

Let's be serious. You're not going to get all that information from one source, and we're not going to give it to you in this book. But we are going to help you find out what internal issues at the top schools often influence who gets accepted. And we're also going to provide you with a powerful set of questions for the admissions officers and financial aid staff at your top-choice colleges so that you'll know how to approach your application knowledgeably.

Adjust Your Thinking—Again

Sorry to tell you this, but if you think that taking the SAT or ACT four or five times to get the highest score, taking every AP class offered in your high school, logging hundreds of hours of community service, being an Eagle Scout, playing five musical instruments, speaking three languages, or holding the patent to a lightbulb that never burns out will get you admitted to one of the schools profiled in this book, think again. If you think that the admissions offices at top-tier colleges are following exactly the same ideals of merit-based admission that you and hundreds of thousands of other college-bound students are following, you're wrong. So why would a college see the process of admitting the best and brightest students differently than you do?

The Business of Managing Enrollment

A lot of people ask enrollment management officers, "How are things in admissions?" This question offers a view into the mindset of those who consider the word "admissions" to sum up what people in enrollment management do. They admit students, don't they? Yes, that's the result that you see, but there's a big difference between what "admissions" and "enrollment" means. Enrollment management refers to a pretty complex system of admitting an appropriate amount of students to a college each year, and, from those admitted, getting the right number of students to matriculate. Think about that for a second. Then answer this question.

> **Q:** If 20,000 students apply for 1,500 seats in a freshman class, how many students should a college accept to make sure that 1,500 actually attend in the fall?

What was your answer? Did you guess 1,500? After all, who would turn down an offer to attend one of the most competitive schools in the nation?

What's the right answer?

> **A:** It depends.

You'd be surprised to learn what factors actually go into making a decision on admittance. Today's enrollment management officers do more than just visit high schools, review applications, and make the tough decisions concerning whom to admit. And financial aid officers don't just consider your Free Application for Federal Student Aid (FAFSA) and send you a financial aid award.

Managing enrollment means satisfying a number of issues that college presidents, boards of trustees and directors, faculty, and others watch carefully every year. These include, but aren't limited to maintaining or increasing the measures of academic quality of incoming students; recruiting student-athletes who will lead the school to a league or division championship; ensuring a balance of students from a variety of cultural and ethnic backgrounds; making sure cocurricular and academic programs like music, art, and theater have students who will fill a second-seat trombone position, paint the next *Mona Lisa*, or end up on (or off) Broadway; assisting college officers with programs to increase retention and graduation rates; recruiting students for under-enrolled academic programs; managing admission into over-enrolled academic programs; and providing adequate net tuition, room, and board revenues, which make up a large portion of the operating budget at most private colleges and universities.

Take it Apart; Put it Back Together

The point here is that admissions and financial aid are both highly complex issues. When things seem very complicated, though, it helps to take apart the issues and look them over one by one. When you have a solid understanding of what goes on in the admissions office and why financial aid and admissions are so closely related from an enrollment manager's perspective, you'll be better prepared to construct a convincing argument for your admission in your applications. You'll be better off than most if you understand what matters inside the admissions office at, say, CalTech, and are able to respond to that in your own unique way.

Remember, each school has its own set of internal circumstances that change every year, which means the admissions criteria change every year. That's why this book isn't about what exactly matters at Duke or Yale or Georgetown. It's about what you need to do, whenever you're applying, to discover what really *is* important to them at that time, address it in your application, and encourage the admissions committee to accept you through other channels as well.

From this point on, you have to stop trying so hard to be admissible on your terms and start learning how to be admissible on real terms that matter to the best colleges in the land.

A Case in Point

A friend of ours (we'll call him Dr. Rhine) came to us a few years ago, obviously agitated and flapping a copy of a letter in our faces. "I can't believe this! My son, Quentin (not his real name), was rejected by Amherst! He's a *great* student. Dartmouth and Brown are looking him over, so why isn't another top, non-Ivy League college interested? Look at this letter!"

We immediately recognized the Amherst letterhead and admissions office signature. "Dr. Rhine, your son wasn't rejected, deferred, or anything of the sort. Take a closer look."

"Of course he was rejected! We planned for months on what he would take in 9th, 10th, 11th, and 12th grade. He took every AP course the school district offered. He got a 5 on the AP History, Chemistry, English, and Calculus tests. He's in the Honors Club. He took the SAT three times, and if you take the highest verbal and math from each test, his SAT composite is a 1570. His GPA, weighted by the school, is a 4.25. He was vice president of his debate club, did *three* Habitat for Humanity projects, and has been a peer tutor in math for the last three years. We looked at Princeton, Yale, Penn, and Swarthmore. We visited Dartmouth and he stayed overnight with two students from the history department, but Quentin fell in love with Yale. We even went back for a second visit, and they really rolled out the red carpet for us!"

"Did Quentin ever apply?"

"Of course he did. He applied to Swarthmore, Amherst, Williams, Dartmouth, Oberlin, Yale, and Brown. We visited Amherst, and the admissions officer seemed very enthusiastic when Quentin expressed an interest in biology and chemistry. In the past few months he has developed an interest in engineering, so he wrote to Amherst and Williams, asking what opportunities they had for a student interested in engineering."

"Well, listen to this sentence:

'We do not feel that our academic programs would be the best match for your specific interests. Accordingly, we strongly encourage you to seek admission to another high-quality college or university that offers engineering…'

"Dr. Rhine, your son hasn't been denied admission. Amherst is just discouraging him from continuing the admissions process because of his desire to study engineering. There are a few other reasons too."

"I can't believe this! Quentin was so pumped up about Amherst, and now he's up in his room, wondering what's wrong with himself. And after all we've done to prepare him for admission, they tell us his academic interests aren't a match for Amherst. That's really strange."

Not really. Over half of all students who enter private colleges today are undecided about their specific majors. This is perfectly natural, and we're used to hearing about how students change their major three or four times before settling on a program. That's partly why we developed a resource for students to learn about majors on www.review.com. But given Quentin's impressive academic and extracurricular record, why would Amherst discourage him from pursuing his application? (Remember, he was neither denied nor granted admission in that letter.) After all, Quentin visited and expressed an interest in biology and chemistry, both of which are strong academic programs at Amherst. Shouldn't they acknowledge that students change majors, and encourage Quentin to visit again and talk things through? Shouldn't they dig deeper into his profile to see what the issues really are?

They did. That's the whole point. You don't know what happened inside the admissions office, but we guarantee it was more than just Quentin's change of initial interest that caused Amherst to send a discouraging letter to him. Dr. Rhine spent the next thirty minutes disbelieving every word we said about why Amherst would discourage anyone from continuing to pursue admission. After all, don't colleges and universities want as many applicants as possible so they can pick the best?

The real issue from his parent's perspective was that Amherst was probably the best place in the world for Quentin. He wanted a small college, a liberal arts atmosphere, but access to engineering. Where better than Amherst, a first-class liberal arts college with ready access to the University of Massachusetts, a major university with a comprehensive engineering program?[1] Or Dartmouth, which interested him greatly for that same reason? (Dartmouth has a bachelor's and a master's degree option in engineering sciences and engineering physics.) Williams, on the other hand, is an equally good undergraduate school but has no engineering program. They told him, however, about all kinds of research available in physics and other professors who would help him with his career in engineering. Amherst's response—that the specific interests Quentin had were not a good match for Amherst—sent a confusing message to him and his parents.

---

[1] Amherst and UMass belong to a consortium, or a group of colleges that allows students enrolled at any of them to take certain classes—usually those unavailable at the student's school—at the others.

What happened to Quentin Rhine? Like many teenagers, he developed a new interest, this one in political science and pre-law. Yale admitted him. His father recently reported, "Quentin is still extremely happy at Yale. He has found that the undergraduate teaching is excellent, he has been extremely pleased with the students he has met there for both their intellectual and cultural diversity, the latter being the distinct difference between Yale and the other schools he looked at..."

Quentin's case points out a variety of issues we'll explore. First, what happened to Quentin at Amherst? Most students would be proud to have his high school record, and most colleges pleased to have him among the freshman class. Second, does it really matter what major you declare when you apply? Of course it does. Finally, what did Amherst know about Quentin—or the Rhine family in particular—that caused the college to dissuade him from seeking admission? If he can get into an Ivy League university but not Amherst, what does that say about the admissions process overall?

Confused?

As aspiring elite college students, high schoolers have been told by teachers, parents, peers, guidance counselors, and admissions officers to do all they can to present the best profile possible when applying to America's top colleges and universities. Yet we see not only denial letters and waitlist notifications, but also the occasional letter discouraging students from continuing the application process at all.

You'll continue to take scholastic assessment tests, volunteer in your community, play sports, join the debate club, take AP and honors-level classes, and even learn to play the tuba—anything to become a well-rounded (at least in admissions terms) applicant.

You'll apply to many colleges, write what you believe is the Great American Novel (your essay), and hope for the best.

The enrollment managers (primarily the admissions and financial aid folks) will use this information (50% of the challenge) and take into account a mind-boggling number of internal and external issues (the other 50%) that go beyond what's in your application. In other words, an admissions office's decision about who gets in and who does not is never based solely on each applicant's portfolio. Did you think it was? If you did, you see now why it's time to adjust your thinking.

Part II

The Quest

Chapter **3**

Preparing for
Excellence

The Parent's Chapter

This chapter is mainly for parents, but you'll probably want to stick your nose in here at least a little bit. Your parents will probably try to discuss this with you anyway, so if you read this chapter, you'll once again come off looking as if you know more than they do when they want to discuss it.

Passion

Passion is a key that can unlock the doors to a top-notch college. The number of parents who haven't figured out what their children's passions are always surprises us. Yeah, they know that their kids have certain obvious talents, but few moms and dads go to the trouble of being really observant. Sometimes passion lies beneath a pile of otherwise mundane activities. So it pays to be a detective.

Your children's formative years will fly by, so pay attention. Don't let the telltale clues of your child's promise slip by unnoticed. Keep a sharp eye out for what lights his or her intellectual fire. What exactly makes your children special? Try to name it. That is, if there were one word to describe your kid's intellectual nature, what would it be? Think of Big Idea words like "balance" and "aesthetic." Once you know what that word is, you'll have taken a big step toward charting a course for his or her future excellence.

In today's college market, the stakes are high and expensive. The smart move is to implement long-range strategies. One of the foundations of any college plan is knowing who the candidate is. If you follow the Temperament Snapshot process (see Chapter 5), you'll begin to find out who your kids are, how they operate, and what their passions are. The bonus may come in finding out who you are along the way.

Wonder Babies

In general, three is the age at which behavioral patterns begin to manifest themselves in children, and an alert parent can start to intuit the key indicators of youthful potential at that age. Wonder Babies are those kids with exceptional promise who eat challenges for lunch.

Plan This

How should you get on with the task of identifying your child's more remarkable characteristics? Here's a simplified parental plan covering age three through middle school.

- Pre-preschool to Elementary Years: Encourage reading and a broad range of interests. Look for signs of special talents. Get involved with your school's guidance program. Start a journal detailing talents you notice in your kid. Play on a computer with him, and when he's old enough, encourage him to work on it by himself. Oh, and read, read, read with him.

- Middle-School Years: Continue reading at more and more challenging levels. Begin to emphasize writing and general communication skills. Watch for emerging leadership traits. Increase your involvement with teachers and administrators. Consider suggesting that your child take the SAT-I to qualify for advanced programs such as the Johns Hopkins Center for Talented Youth.

- High School Years: Don't be surprised if your advice or enthusiasm annoys your child. If the passion for learning that you've tried to develop in her has taken root by the time she gets through middle school, you probably won't have to encourage her to get involved in activities that will broaden her horizons.

As a matter of fact, you might have to switch roles to help her understand that she shouldn't overextend herself with countless extras in high school.

Vicarious Kid Syndrome

Let's talk about motivations. Have you ever thought, "Hey, I never had the chance to go to a highly selective, expensive college when I was a kid. So now my kid's gonna get that chance"? If you have, you may be suffering from Vicarious Kid Syndrome. You may be trying to relive your life through your kid. Do not do this. Don't try to force your kid to fulfill your dream. You have to ask yourself a hard question, "Do I want my kid to go to an elite school so that the prestige (whatever that means) will rub off on me?" Be honest. You're reading this in private and no one is impatiently waiting for your answer. You don't have to attend a VKSers Anonymous meeting, stand up, and say, "Hello. My name is Joe Bloggs, and I want to live vicariously through my kid." Just be aware of your stance here.

After careful thought, if you believe that your son or daughter truly has competitive potential for the crème de la crème of American colleges, then you should become an advocate for his or her desire to attend. But think about that: it has to be your child's desire. If your intention to help your kid succeed is rooted anywhere near your own self-interests, you're gambling with his long-range happiness and college success.

Observe your kid with as objective an eye as possible. If he's competitive, advocate some top colleges. That's all. Notice that the message is not "Dedicate your life to getting your kid into the most prestigious college possible, come hell or high water." There's a big difference. Don't substitute your own aspirations for those of your kid. He'll have a hard enough time living his own life.

The Usual Real-Life Example

Try employing a journal of your kid's achievements and development. Here are some brief excepts from one parent's journal whose child we'll call Graham. Graham ended up getting into one of the finest undergraduate schools in the nation. We've put this here to give you an idea of how you can use such a tool to discern your own child's passion.

Age 1–2: Graham is spending lots of time with books, as listener, observer, and sometimes participant. Susan (Graham's mother) and I seem to be constantly feeding G's hunger for books and words. Susan brings home simple puzzle books from the grocery store every week. G. works them from front to back and then waits for the next one. Great interest in verbal skills.

Age 3: First home computer [Atari 800]. Graham attracted like a magnet. Games at first, then as reading skills manifest, interest in my *Compute* magazines. We read articles on games and new computer products. Moved from puzzle books to logic-game books. More books, library trips, and intro to classical music. Reading, words, puzzles, and construction toys (Transformers and Legos) fill his days.

Age 4: G. has figured out an original keyboarding technique. It's not touch-typing but it's very fast. Don't know where it came from. Typing in game programs from *Compute*. Every character has to be perfect or program won't run. Frustrating, but he persists until successful. Saves games on cassette tapes. More books. Bought a telescope and am teaching G. the Messier numbers of planetary nebulae as we spot them.

Age 5: Preschool. Bought G. a book on 6502 processor assembler language. Wrote assembler mnemonics on flash cards and made a game out of them. Only 5-year-old in town who knows these, I'll bet. G. wrote poem at school, "The Red Ghost." Principal read it to students at an assembly. G. is writing a lot of stuff in little notebooks.

> Elementary years: Writing simple computer games. Began gifted-support curriculum (1st grade). Qualified for advanced math programs. Odyssey of the Mind World Finals (6th grade). State finals Mathcounts competition. Orchestra (4th grade on saxophone).

And so on. Seem like Graham has a passion for computers or math? If you're an especially observant parent, you may want to continue your journal through the middle- and high-school years. The value of a journal like this is the detail it can recall. How many of us can remember all the little anecdotes of our kids' lives? And it doesn't take a lot of effort to create and maintain a journal. They can be priceless, however, when it comes times to say a word on behalf of your kids at college application time. (Yes, some colleges out there will entertain recommendations from parents and even provide standardized forms for it). Perhaps that may be these journals' biggest advantage.

Public Schools, Private Schools, and Kitchen Tables

Both a parent's and student's experience with public schooling revolves around where they live. If you live in a district where the schools are well funded and the teaching is fantastic, then you're more likely to have a positive experience than you would if you live in a lower-income district. Even lower-income schools can have their bright spots, though. It's up to parents to find the opportunities within these schools and exploit them.

The public-school parent's mantra must be "Get involved." This involvement begins on Day One in preschool and persists through kindergarten, the elementary years, and up through middle school and high school to graduation. You may think that your child's fourteen-year-long, precollege education window is a long haul, but it flies by incredibly fast. The bottom line on public schools is that many times, they are what you make of them. Assuming that you have hatched a Wonder Baby, don't just shuttle him or her off into your local public system and hope for the best. Be a good consumer. Check it out, check with other parents, and—most of all—stay involved.

The private-school route offers both edges of the sword. Don't be misled into thinking that just because you pay tens of thousands of dollars for a private educational experience that it's going to guarantee success. The primary advantages of the private route over the public route are (1) the quality of curriculum and its delivery (teaching quality), (2) the likelihood of personal relationships emerging between students and faculty, and (3), in the end, better overall college counseling.

The boarding or day-student decision can be crucial, depending on your kid's need for interaction with you.

Chapter 4

Targeting the Top

Cachet

In 1999, the eight Ivy League schools combined received over 121,000 applications. That doesn't include the likes of Stanford, Rice, Georgetown, MIT, Duke, or the rest of the schools profiled in this book. There was space for about 12% of these kids. Why would so many people apply to so few schools? Brand awareness. In the high-end world of personal stuff, you have BMW, Mercedes Benz, Gucci, Rolex, and so on. Just the mention of those names commands immediate attention. It works the same way with the name of an elite college.

Mike Marshland/Yale University Photographer

Yale University, or "Yale College" as it is sometimes called, is among America's oldest and most quintessential "Ivy" schools. With its classic Gothic architecture and twelve residential colleges, student living takes on a traditional European ambiance. Yale's 5,300 undergraduates enjoy comfortable classes too. Nearly 85% of courses enroll fewer than 25 people, 40% enroll fewer than ten, and faculty are very accessible.

It's called cachet. It's okay to want to go to Brown or Harvard, but you, the student, had better be able to justify your desires. Parents, it's the same story for you. If you push your kids to go elite for the snob appeal, well, you just might end up with snobs for children and a bunch of rejection letters in your mailbox.

Don't let your parents do your college selection for you. Think for yourself. Beyond that, don't target any college for the wrong reasons, like "Notre Dame is where so-and-so from *Buffy* is going" or "I read this really cool story about the crazy parties at Dartmouth." Sure, it's cool to apply to HYPSM (that stands for Harvard, Yale, Princeton, Stanford, and MIT). But it could be even cooler if you applied to a different HYPSM (Hamilton, Yeshiva, Pomona, Scripps, and Macalester) for the right reasons.

College-Pick Logic and Other Mysteries

Most families spend more time selecting their living-room furniture than they do evaluating colleges. High school students are especially evasive in articulating their selection criteria. They've been known to invoke more than a bit of twisted logic.

Here are ten reasons why kids pick certain colleges (we've heard all of these at one time or another):

1. "My boyfriend/girlfriend is going there."

2. "They had a national championship football/ basketball/hockey/etc. team last year."

3. "It's close to/far from home."

4. "There are lots of black/Jewish/Catholic/gay/ lesbian/Latin/Asian/etc. students there."

5. "It's Harvard/Yale/Princeton/Stanford/MIT/Duke/ Williams/etc."

6. "They offered such a good aid package, my parents could buy me a car."

7. "My brother/sister/father/mother/grandfather/ grandmother/aunt/uncle/etc. went there."

8. "The guys/girls/buildings/campus/etc. in their viewbook looked so cool."

9. "I like to ski/surf/climb/swim/hang glide/play Ultimate Frisbee/etc."

10. "It meets more of my criteria than most other colleges."

Guess which one makes the most sense. We know that you know the answer to this one. To be thorough, however, let's address each one.

From the list above, you can see a number of irrelevant things being considered. Since the focus of this book is elite colleges, let's start with #5: "It's Harvard/Yale/Princeton/Stanford/MIT/Duke/Williams/etc."

With these schools' reputations, it's not hard to understand why you might develop a passion for one or all of them based solely on perception. As with anything you buy, like TVs and cars, choosing a well-known and well-respected brand name is relatively safe, but it's not entirely risk-free. There are easy ways to verify the overall quality of a brand-name college if you're willing to do a little work.

Two direct methods work best: reading the student newspaper and communicating with people there. Just about every college publishes a student-run newspaper and most are available on the web. Student newspapers are famous for telling it like it is, so much so that sometimes college administrators forbid publication of certain articles or opinion pieces. They have been known to go around campus gathering up the offending publications, and even burning them. Sound like the Inquisition? Well, college administrators worry about image too.

At any rate, if you're looking to find out what any of the best colleges out there are like, search the web for "college newspapers" and you'll be pleased to find *The Yale Daily News*, *The Brown Daily Herald*, *The Stanford Daily*, *The Dartmouth*, *The Daily Pennsylvanian*, *The Rice Thresher*, *The Columbia Daily Spectator*, and those of all of the other elite colleges. Uwire.com reports campus news from all around the country. Read these sources carefully. Is the school they describe a place you want to be?

You also want to know what the students who go there think. Start with the profiles in the back of this book. We've included the opinions of thousands of students who responded to our surveys about academics at these schools. You could also check out www.review.com for more extensive information on all aspects of life—from the student perspective—at these schools and others.

Many college websites provide links to student web pages. These are gold mines of insight into a college's flavor and character. If you want to know the general feel of a student body, check out about a half-dozen or so of these. You'll find everything from pictures of students, their friends, families, and pets, to their roommates and beyond.

Once you've browsed your candidate schools, it's time to make contact. Be prepared in advance, though. Don't just send an e-mail to someone whom you never met and say something like, "Hey, dude, your web page is really cool. What's it like at Penn, anyway?" Can you guess what's wrong with this approach?

Well, for starters, that question is just too broad. Be specific. Before you make contact, write down your top-five list of questions about that school. You might want to know about a certain major (most students list their majors on their pages). You may want to find out about that highly touted "12-to-1 student-to-teacher ratio" by asking your newly found student contact if she has had many teaching assistants in class. Ask about the food, the computer resources, the dorms, the parties, weekends on campus, the local town or city, available transportation, cost of living, weather, sports—whatever is important to you—but have your five or so questions ready before you write that e-mail.

And the Other Nine

The thinking behind these reasons falls into four general categories. Remember, some kids make their college picks based on things other than what their own heads and hearts tell them. And there's mom and dad, of course, who might be providing strong input that stems from any number of motivations, selfish or otherwise. Here are the four general categories:

Possibly temporal personal reasons

Attitudes and cyclical fads come and go. That's why picking a college based on reasons from this group can be dangerous (and expensive). The five here are just a sampling; there are other variations. Think about these for a minute, though:

> "My boyfriend/girlfriend is going there."

Don't be stupid. Enough said about that.

> "They had a national championship football/basketball/hockey/etc. team last year."

Ever heard the phrase "from the penthouse to the outhouse"? This happens a lot in the world of sports. It's easy to be "Notre Dame Proud" when the Irish gridiron squad is 11-1 or 12-0. How proud will you be after two consecutive .500 or (heaven forbid) losing seasons? Sure, there are perennial sports powerhouses out there, but their continuing dominance isn't ever certain. Coaches retire, get fired, and have bad recruiting years. You had better be sure that you can survive your college's "outhouse" days.

"It's close to/far from home."

"I like to ski/surf/climb/swim/hang glide/play Ultimate Frisbee/etc."

You may feel that right now you just have to get as far away as possible from mom, dad, and your brothers and sisters. Like all feelings, this one's subject to change. If you live in New Jersey and pick a college in Oregon, you're going to experience lots of hassles if, after you spend a few weeks away from the old homestead, you find that the folks back home weren't all that bad.

The flip-side of this feeling is the need to be not that far away from friends and family. That's fine, too. On the other hand, if you're unwilling to leave home, you may be skipping out on an important lesson in maturity and independence. College is a chance to steer your life in new directions. Keep an open mind.

Picking a college simply because surf's up, the powder is close to the clam chowder, or whatever, is another of these conditional choices. Conditions can change. If you pick a school in the far Northeast for skiing opportunities and then lose interest, you could discover just how cold New Hampshire winters really are when you're not careening down a slalom at full speed. Then there are the low-snow winters when the powder is scarce and the mud's plentiful. Just examine your geographic preferences carefully before committing to a school.

> "The guys/girls/buildings/campus/etc. in their viewbook looked so cool."

This one's the worst. Take out a bunch of the viewbooks you've been sent—any of them—and look at them all at once. See any similarities? Notice how just about every college has buildings sporting high Gothic spires and a good dose of ivy growing in all the right places? The lawns are a lush green and the sky is a deep blue with just a touch of fluffy white clouds. There's usually a lake, beside which a distinguished-looking professor leads his very small class in a discussion of some profound topic. Best of all, the students are so diverse.

Middlebury College

Viewbooks are marketing pieces. When was the last time you saw a Whopper coming at you through the drive-up window that looked like a Whopper on a television commerical? It's the same thing with viewbooks. Go and visit these places if they interest you. Look for that lake. Is it drained? Check out those Gothic spires. Is the building still inhabited by humans? What about those small classes? Are they for real? What's the statistical breakdown of minorities in the student body? Maybe they put the entire minority population into that one picture.

Almighty dollar reasons
"They offered such a good aid package, my parents could buy me a car."

As incredible as it may sound, financial considerations shouldn't always be first on your list. Less-than-great college experiences happen more often because of money than for any other reason. Don't let sticker price alone be your criterion. Take our word for it. We'll tell you more about this a little later.

Personal pride and family-tradition reasons
"There are lots of black/Jewish/Catholic/gay/ lesbian/Latin/Asian/etc. students there."

"My brother/sister/father/mother/grandfather/ grandmother/aunt/uncle/etc. went there."

Picking a college because your family members went there or because others "like you" go there may greatly limit your personal growth. Even though your relatives may have found one particular school that met their unique needs, that school might not do the same for you. Likewise, if you want to stay around other people whose backgrounds, in whatever aspect, are the same as your own, then a school with many similar kinds of students should be fine.

Keep in mind, though, that it's a big world out there and you'll eventually have to enter the fray. And since you often won't be able to control the kind of people you'll be around, it may be better to consider a broader range of college demographic options.

The Best Reason

"It meets more of my criteria than most other colleges."

There may be other ways of stating it, but this is by far the best approach to picking a college. It covers all the bases: demographics, location, financial considerations, and so forth. Approaching college selection with a mind toward balance is similar to having a smart investment strategy. If you spread your investment across several different kinds of holdings, an isolated downturn in the stock market can't hurt you that badly. When you're picking a school, the one that fulfills most of your criteria (even if it isn't the absolute best in any of them) will without a doubt provide you with the best overall college experience.

Chapter 5

The Temperament Snapshot

We're not going to go off on a tangent here blabbering on about arcane head-shrinking theories. What we are going to do is give you an easy-to-take, short course on understanding yourself better.

NOTE TO PARENTS: Keep reading. You'll benefit from this discussion too. In fact, if everyone in your family over the age of fourteen does a Temperament Snapshot, you'll all end up understanding one another a whole lot better.

The goal here is to help you understand what your temperament is so that you can convincingly communicate who you are and what you're all about in your application. This increased knowledge of self will allow you to sharpen your argument as to why a certain college is the best choice for you. That's the kind of stuff admissions committees love to read.

What Exactly is Temperament?

You've all heard someone say something like, "Oh, yes! She's got a great temperament for a [nurse, accountant, scientist, stuntman, writer, whatever]." Well, what is it that makes a person right for what she's doing? It's all about behavioral preferences.

By the time we become teenagers, we all develop certain favorite ways of doing things. We become increasingly predictable about how we'll react in certain situations. Those reactions define our behaviors. The fact that we repeat those behaviors shows that we prefer them, as if they are instinctive. In fact, they really are instinctive. The phrase "behavioral preferences" merely means "the way we like to live our lives."

Let's start with the six traits. Each is represented by a letter.

S = realism	N = dreaming
T = analysis	F = sympathy
J = planning	P = improvisation

These six basic traits, or behavioral preferences, form in pairs inside our brains. We all tend to prefer one or the other of a trait from each horizontal pair in the columns above. That is, in most situations, we consistently prefer, for example, realism to dreaming, sympathy to analysis, or planning to improvisation.

You're One of a Kind

The four pairs are: NF, NT, SJ, and SP. There is no order of importance; they're all equally important. We just put them in alphabetical order. NF stands for the *Idealist*, NT is the *Rational*, SJ is the *Guardian*, and SP is the *Artisan*. For the curious, "S" stands for "Sensing," "N" stands for "iNtution," "T" stands for "Thinking," "F" stands for "Feeling," "J" stands for "Judging," and "P" stands for "Perceiving."

What will you get out of the ten-minute investment it takes to do a Temperament Snapshot? First, you'll learn which of the four temperaments you are. Second, once you know which pair of letters applies to you, you'll be able to use this information to help you find not only better candidate colleges, but also possibly the right major. As a bonus, you may even be able to confirm which careers may be best suited to bring you success and happiness. Obviously, knowing all this before you start your application essays will make writing about yourself a lot easier and even enjoyable. The bottom line is that you'll come out of this exercise knowing a lot more about yourself and your possible future than you did coming in.

Twenty-one Questions and a Ballpark

Take the Snapshot when you're not tired or stressed out. It's not all that big a deal, but your frame of mind can affect your responses. Ideally, you should be relaxed when you pick your answers. Keep in mind that there are no right or wrong answers here, only *your* answers. Don't think about your answers. Pick the one that appeals to you first. Don't go back and change your answers once you've made a choice. As far as scoring, follow the simple A-B-C prompts on the answer sheet.

Temperament Snapshot

For most of these questions, imagine yourself as a college student. When answering the questions, check "a" or "b" in the appropriately numbered box on the answer sheet, and then score your results.

1. You're doing an experiment for your freshman physics class. As you work, do you

   (a) feel more comfortable executing each step in proper sequence, or

   (b) want to skip the preliminaries, forge ahead, and maybe work in some shortcuts?

2. Your roommate asks you to read a short story he has written for a creative writing course. After reviewing it, do you first

   (a) point out the areas that need to be improved, or

   (b) mention the parts that you liked?

3. Based on the way you approached other major projects in high school, how would you characterize your approach to your college application process? Will you:

   (a) organize your tasks, make a schedule, and mail everything on time, or did/will you

   (b) put off a lot of the work until the last minute, maybe even enjoying the pressure?

4. You go to the campus art museum and encounter a large wall covered by many small, individually hung paintings. As you first look at them, do you

   (a) examine many details of each, noticing their subjects, colors, and brushstrokes, or

   (b) ponder their arrangement on the wall, noticing the display's balance and symmetry?

5. You are a member of your college's student disciplinary council. The latest case involves a student who claims the damage he did to his room was due to a self-defense struggle he had with an unidentified assailant. There were no witnesses, but the student tells a convincing story. During council deliberations, do you tend to give more weight to

   (a) the fact that school regulations have been violated, or

   (b) the student's apparently extenuating circumstances?

6.   Your anthropology professor has been promising your class a reading list and schedule of assignments since classes began two weeks ago. Due to this lack of planning information, do you

   (a)   feel unsettled and off balance, or

   (b)   indifferent?

7.   You face a tough decision about an important senior-year project on which you're working. In making your decision, do you rely more on

   (a)   your past experience in situations similar to this, or

   (b)   your hunches about what the best thing to do is?

8.   In deciding which elective courses to take in order to fulfill your degree requirements, are your final choices influenced more by

   (a)   which ones appear to best serve your career goals, or

   (b)   which ones you seem to like best?

9.   One of your Speech Communications course requirements is to choose and deliver (in front of your class) one of two types of five-minute presentations. Do you prefer

   (a)   the one that allows for advanced planning, or

   (b)   the improvisational one, where you make it up as you go?

10.   You're the campaign manager for this year's underdog in the race for student-senate president. Would you say that the vast majority of your strategies will be

   (a)   sensible, realistic, and practical, or

   (b)   inspired, clever, and imaginative?

11.   In your senior year, you work as a teaching assistant for your psychology professor. On the day that a critical class report is due, one of the freshman from the class tells you that his report isn't ready because he was up all night at his dying grandmother's bedside. Is your first instinct to

   (a)   apply some kind of grade penalty for lateness and give him a revised deadline, or

   (b)   understand his circumstances and ask him when he could have the report completed?

12. Several weeks before moving to campus for your first year of college, you have a chance to meet your new roommate. S/he asks you to tell her/him a little bit about yourself. Would your description more likely include words such as

    (a) structured, orderly, decisive, and controlled, or

    (b) spontaneous, open, going with the flow, and somewhat indecisive?

13. While trying to decide whether or not to take a graduate-level course in your junior year, do you give more weight to

    (a) the actual amount of work involved, or

    (b) the possible advantages of taking it?

14. You've been asked to serve as a student representative on your college's fundraising committee. When volunteering for specific subcommittees, do you prefer to

    (a) be a strategist and devise and analyze the best fundraising plans, or

    (b) offer insights about who might be the best people to approach for contributions?

15. As far as showing up for your classes is concerned, do you find yourself

    (a) arriving early most of the time, or

    (b) dashing in at the last minute, sometimes late, or occasionally not showing up at all?

16. You and your roommate are discussing which of two movies to go see. Do you cast your vote for

    (a) the historical documentary, or

    (b) the science-fiction fantasy?

17. You've heard the campaign speeches of your class's presidential candidates. One candidate is very charismatic and likeable, but his platform is weaker than that of his opponent, whose personality is less agreeable. Is your vote influenced more by

    (a) the relative reasonability of the candidates' platform promises, or

    (b) your personal reaction to their respective personalities?

18. Yesterday, your chemistry professor instructed your lab partner to select an appropriate semester project for you two. As for your partner's selection process, do you want to

    (a) get the show on the road and have him choose a project now, or

    (b) wait and see what might turn up, keeping the options open?

19. You and a classmate are discussing the successes and difficulties you've both experienced in a tough calculus course so far this semester. As you talk about your own performance, does your assessment emphasize

    (a) your actual test-score average to date, or

    (b) your prediction as to your possible future test results?

20. Three of your friends with whom you were planning to go to the football game change their minds at the last minute and now say they want you to go on a road trip with them. Do you

    (a) ask, "Why the sudden change in plans?", or

    (b) agree to go with them rather than cause a fuss?

21. In thinking about how your dorm friends, classmates, and professors view you, would you say that they might describe you with words like

    (a) task-oriented, driven, planner, and scheduler, or

    (b) procrastinator, open-ended, tentative, flexible, and adaptable?

Temperament Snapshot Answer Sheet

	a.	b.		a.	b.		a.	b.
1.			2.			3.		
4.			5.			6.		
7.			8.			9.		
10.			11.			12.		
13.			14.			15.		
16.			17.			18.		
19.			20.			21.		
A. Totals:	S	N		T	F		J	P

B. Letter of higher score:

C. Circle the one pair of letters that contains two of your three letters:

NF   SP

NT   SJ

Now we're going to put the puzzle pieces together. Let's say that the results of your Snapshot show that you are an NF. Using the trait words, we see that two qualities combine to form your temperament: dreaming and sympathy. The designation for NF is idealist.

Idealists seek meaning and significance in all that they do. Their values include an instinctive and high regard for ethics and morality, authenticity, cooperation, unity, and personal relationships. Some of their unique roles include that of the romantic idealist, counselor, diplomat, and mentor.

You'll see idealists display such behaviors as imagination, empathy, praise, warm-heartedness, and spirituality. They are relationship-oriented, use metaphorical language, have vivid imaginations, and can become deeply involved in whatever they're doing.

If your letters are NT, you are among the rationals. Rationals seek to gain knowledge and competence in all that they do. They want to have power over nature. They value intelligence, progress, scientific inquiry, and theory. They seek expert relationships and embrace concepts and ideas. Logic and consistency is at or near the top of their lists. Roles and skills of the rational include that of the engineer and inventor. They are lifelong learners and visionaries, analyzing and strategizing master designs.

Rationals organize projects well. They display precision in speech, and tend to be coldly logical, cynical, and analytical. They like to work, and they love to solve problems. They can be perfectionists and highly critical of themselves. For rationals, everything can always be improved.

Those of you with the SJ designation are guardians. Guardians are highly responsible and dedicated to whatever duties they are performing. They value rules and regulations, stability, security, and conformity. Guardians (surprise!) are the protectors in our world. They think sequentially and supervise, measure, monitor, and stabilize situations at home, work, and in social situations. They're great at logistics when things need to be organized.

Guardians have a high regard for authority and respect the hierarchy of the chain of command. They are upset when others display a blatant disregard for rules and regulations. Guardians use customary language. They often tend to be somewhat negative or fatalistic in their outlook. The author of Murphy's Law had to have been a guardian. They are responsible, cautious, meticulous, structured, and economical. Guardians are rock-solid and dependable.

Are you an SP? If so, you're an artisan. Artisans are the impact people in our world. They need freedom to act on their impulses and their ability to make strong impressions. "I gotta be free to be me" would be a good artisan motto. They seek the thrill of action and risk, with the action being the end in itself.

People who get to know Artisans often describe them as fun-loving, upbeat, sometimes intense, and always exciting to be around. The fact that artisans tend to live outside of the rules gives them this stimulating aura. To observe artisans at work, simply look to the arts and sports. Michael Jordan, Andre Agassi, John Lennon, Ernest Hemingway, and many other big-name personalities are artisans.

How Does This Relate to College and Me?

Once you know what temperament you are, you can find out which career fields are the most popular among many other people with your temperament. This can help you narrow down the types of work that would most likely bring you success and/or happiness. The converse is also true: You can also see which fields attract and retain the fewest people with temperaments like yours. Obviously, you may find these fields are less appealing (although not necessarily so).

Just because you want to be marine biologist, for example, and that particular field does not appear among the most popular for your temperament, don't for a minute think that you shouldn't follow your dreams. Think of temperament as a way of getting into a ballpark, not necessarily as a way of finding your specific seat. It is a general guideline, not permission to follow only one career or college path.

Here are the most and least popular occupations for the four temperaments.

Most popular careers for the Idealist (NF)
Teachers of music, art, and drama; writers; priests; physicians; psychologists; vocational and educational counselors; educational consultants; journalists; social workers; musicians and composers; editors and reporters; speech pathologists; designers; and high school teachers

Least popular careers for the Idealist (NF)
Police and detectives; farmers; sales managers; steelworkers; factory supervisors; service workers; bank officers; financial managers; chemical engineers; computer systems analysts; corrections officers; electronic technicians; mathematics teachers; auditors; credit investigators; and real-estate agents and brokers

---

Most popular careers for the Rational (NT)
Attorneys; photographers; systems analysts; actors; credit investigators; mortgage brokers; physical scientists; social scientists; computer programmers; judges; sales managers; chemical engineers; research assistants; writers; marketing personnel; electronic technicians; university teachers; and computer specialists

Least popular careers for the Rational (NT)
Teachers' aides; cashiers; receptionists; nurses; bookkeepers; mining engineers; typists; steelworkers; factory and site supervisors; public service aides; guards; home economists; library attendants; secretaries; religious educators; elementary-school teachers; hair dressers; health-service workers; and clerical supervisors

Most popular careers for the Guardian (SJ)
Teachers; preachers; accountants; bankers; clerks; nurses; rehabilitation therapists; insurance agents; managers; sales executives; service occupations; secretaries; general-practice physicians; dentists; barbers; pharmacists; and librarians

Least popular careers for the Guardian (SJ)
Actors; psychiatrists; lawyers; computer system analysts; electricians; marketing personnel; photographers; writers; psychologists; editors; reporters; education consultants; social scientists; designers; restaurant workers; counselors; musicians; composers; resident-housing assistants; speech pathologists; and mining engineers

Most popular careers for the Artisan (SP)
Performers in the arts; race-car drivers; construction workers; heavy-equipment operators; loggers; freight-dock workers; event promoters; ambulance drivers; surfers; mercenaries; negotiators; entrepreneurs; professional athletes; bellhops; and bartenders

Least popular careers for the Artisan (SP)
Chemical engineers; psychiatrists; mechanical engineers; research workers; education consultants; electronic technicians; dental hygienists; food-counter workers; journalists; clerical supervisors; nurses; preschool teachers; priests; public-relations workers; and medical assistants

For the purposes of your applications, you ought to know what your temperament is and how that projects into a likely field for your life's work. We've just skimmed the surface here, but you now probably know more about who you are and how you can contribute to your community than most other prospective college applicants (or even parents of prospective college applicants). Don't put all of your eggs into the temperament basket, though. Use this information as just one more valuable piece of information about who you are.

Chapter 6

Strategies and Tactics

It's time to take a long look at the college-admission process from a different angle by figuring out the reasons you are applying to an elite college, connecting those reasons with a college's internal needs and wants, and developing a strategy for communicating with those on the inside who might prove to be advocates during your application process.

Most colleges understand that students and their families shop around for a college as they would shop for a car. Keep in mind, though, that America's top schools are in a seller's market. There are simply tens of thousands more applications to these schools than there are seats each year. You still want to apply to the colleges that make the most sense for you personally, not just seek admission at any of the top schools simply for the name. Think for a moment how much more convincing an application you'll put together when you know the reasons (and can spell them out) behind your decision to apply to Whatever University.

Now is the time to (a) narrow the choices of colleges you wish to consider, (b) develop a sense of why these choices are appropriate for you, and (c) plan a systematic approach for learning all you can about how these schools gather information about you and then make their decisions about who is right for *them.* High school and independent college counselors are excellent advocates during this process, and campus visits are absolutely necessary.

America's Top Colleges and You

The process of determining which college is the best for you includes six important steps:

1. Examining the features of a degree that are important to you.

2. Determining which schools provide degrees with those features.

3. Finding out how a school delivers most of its academic programs.

4. Finding out who teaches classes, labs, and lectures.

5. Identifying what is unique about a college.

6. Getting a bottom line net cost figure for attending the school.

Let's tackle the first five first. We'll discuss the net cost of attending your top-choice colleges in Chapter 11.

Prestige

If a college's prestigious reputation is important to you, ask yourself what you believe prestige can do to help you succeed academically, personally, or professionally. Do you believe you'll make more money if you attend a prestigious college? Or do you want to run a Fortune 500 corporation by the time you are thirty years old? It's time to see through the stereotypes and get a sense of what is really important to you, understand why, and then seek out the real attributes and principles that our nation's top schools embrace. Here are a few ways, though not the only ways, to think this through.

Personal Assessment—What You Want
Out of Your College Experience

What do you want to do with your degree? If you want to go to graduate school to earn an MBA, for example, you should target a college with a track record for getting students into good business schools. There is no guarantee that students from prestigious colleges with average or below-average academic records will get accepted into graduate schools any more easily than will students with excellent academic records from lesser-known colleges. This includes the Ivy League graduate who wishes to continue graduate studies at his or her alma mater. You still have to achieve a superior academic record if you go to an Ivy League school.

What are the kinds of careers to which you seem to be attracted? Do you want to help people as a social worker? Or do you want to work on the next generation of space stations? You'll want to investigate a top college that offers the major or interdisciplinary program (courses bundled together from complementary departments) that provides the courses you'll need and the faculty who can help you match your personality, learning style, and skills with potential career choices once you've graduated.

Will a degree in your field from the college you're considering offer you an advantage you can count on when you go looking for a job? Simply having an engineering program with a list of famous graduates, many of whom went on to run their own companies, is no guarantee that you'll be assured preference in a job hunt with those corporations. All colleges have someone you'd probably recognize as having made it big in some field. What you want to know is whether these alumni show preference for graduates from their alma mater. If so, how do you tap into their companies? What are the gateways, and whom do you talk to in order to find out which courses, programs, internships, and other experiences they'll value from your college?

The bottom line is that you should seek out colleges that specialize in preparing you for a particular graduate program, career choice, or help you develop a specific set of skills that you'll need in the future. Don't be lured into a college because of the perception of prestige. Ask the college to introduce you to the people who teach the classes or to those who perform the research in which you're interested. No matter what top college you're accepted to, you want the very best faculty who research and teach undergraduates.

Of course, you might be one of those many applicants accepted as an undeclared major, and that's completely okay. If that's the case, however, a lot of the aforesaid still holds true. You've a better chance of finding your passion when you're in close contact with people who were so passionate about a subject that they studied it enough to earn the highest degree possible in it.

Liberal Arts Colleges vs. Research Universities: What's the Difference?

According to the Carnegie Foundation, a private philanthropic group located in New York, research universities offer a full range of baccalaureate programs, are committed to graduate education through the doctorate degree, and receive a minimum of $15 million in federal research support. Liberal arts colleges, on the other hand, place a major emphasis on baccalaureate degree programs, and many award at least 40% of their degrees in a liberal arts field. But is this the only difference?

Generally, research universities are large, located in cities or urban areas, focus on research at the graduate level, employ a faculty and staff that's sometimes the size of a small town's population, and enroll up to 50,000 students. Liberal arts colleges are usually smaller (anywhere from 500 to 5,000 students), focus on teaching undergraduate students, and offer more opportunities for undergraduates to assist professors with their research.

Most liberal arts colleges require students to take many more courses in "traditional" subjects such as history, languages, communications, philosophy, psychology, and other subjects as part of a core curriculum that all students must take. Many research universities tend to be more specialized in a particular field and require fewer of these traditional courses.

The most important differences for many students and their families is that most liberal arts colleges offer more flexibility in their curriculum and provide more personal attention and direct faculty contact than do research universities.

At Penn, for example, classes can exceed sixty students for an upper-class course, and 500 in a lecture class. At a smaller school such as Dartmouth, classes tend to be much smaller. It does affect your experience, despite the Ivy label of both. The bottom line is that if you just want Ivy or elite for a label, you're being superficial, and no matter what the name on the door, programs and missions do differ among the top schools. For example, Swarthmore is vastly different from Harvard. One is a small liberal arts college, the other a world-class research institution.

The boughs of Swarthmore College arboretum's trees shade the path leading to the admissions office. With a student body of just over 1,400, Swarthmore is small but mighty, perennially among America's top handful of liberal arts colleges. "Swat" is rooted in the Quaker tradition and famous for its academic rigor, fervent faculty, and diversity. The school's $1 billion endowment provides resources that are out of reach for most other similarly sized colleges. In light of all it offers, it's no wonder that gaining admission is becoming increasingly difficult.

Beyond College Brochures: Ten Powerful Questions to Ask

The following ten questions are designed to help you move beyond the general messages in college brochures and provide you with clear, useful answers to essential questions.

1. Which programs represent the core of a college's academic offerings? This question can take many forms, like: What is a college really known for, an academic program, or a unique major? Georgetown, for instance, is well-known and respected for its international relations programs, while Cooper Union is famous for its engineering. Other versions of this question might be which classes are taught that distinguish the program from others? Are there special internships or study-abroad opportunities that seem to match your desires? If so, are you going to be able to take part in these experiences during your four years, and under what circumstances?

2. How are academic programs taught? Are they in large classes, small labs, or unique locations? Are there distance learning facilities? Are small class discussions the norm? Are you required to read a few textbooks, take a test or two, and write a few papers to get your grade, or are there other approaches that complement your learning style?

3. Will you participate in undergraduate research? Whether in the sciences, humanities, or other liberal arts fields, make sure your top college choice offers hands-on learning. Potential employers and graduate admissions officers take a longer look at prospects who have already demonstrated research proficiency in their fields of study.

4. Who teaches? Who will provide teaching and mentoring in your classes, labs, lectures, and other academic experiences? Are faculty full-time, part-time, or adjunct professors? Do teaching assistants handle lectures or small discussion groups? Some adjunct faculty can be quite effective at teaching special courses, and are often alumni who are professionals in their fields. Ask for the credentials of those who would be teaching in your area of interest.

Inside Tip

Log on to a college's website. Find the student newspaper and look for letters, editorials, or features that speak about new programs and majors. If you discover that your college of choice is developing a new program or is looking to fill seats in a major, you should call the department chairperson, talk about your interests, and make an appointment to visit his or her office and facilities. Make sure the admissions office knows you were there. Ask the faculty member to send a note to the admissions office referencing your visit.

5. Can the college give you examples of how professors are accessible to students? Most professors set aside a few hours each week for appointments with students. You need to know more. A professor's life in a university isn't limited to teaching you, grading your papers, and spending an hour discussing your work in his or her office once a month. Ask current students when, where, and why they interact with faculty outside class. You can also check out professor availability ratings in *The Best 331 Colleges.*

6. What is the school's student/faculty ratio? Here's a question you shouldn't ask. This is a statistic that rarely describes how many students actually sit in class with a faculty member.

Inside Tip

The student/faculty ratio is usually computed by first adding all registered undergraduate student credit hours for a particular semester or academic year. Next, colleges use a term called the "full-time equivalent student," or FTE. The minimum number of credit hours needed per semester to be considered matriculated as a full-time, rather than part-time, student defines an FTE student. Many colleges use twelve credit hours, (three four-credit courses, four three-credit courses, or some equivalent combination). Divide the total registered credit hours by the minimum credits needed for full-time status, and you end up with the total number of FTE students at a college. Finally, divide the total number of full-time faculty teaching that semester or year into the total FTE number, and you end up with the student/faculty ratio. Some colleges include other faculty, such as part-time or adjunct professors teaching that semester or academic year.

7. What is unique about this college? If five schools on your list all are perceived as having great programs in biology, how can you tell which is the best choice for you? While most schools may list biology as a popular major, you need to know if the biology department has regular equipment updates, strong endowment support for undergraduate research and scholarships that offset the cost of tuition, alumni who have undertaken important scientific research to which undergraduates are

directly exposed, or plans for growth in the near future. Bottom line: find out why biology is strong, but never ask any college to compare itself to another school.

8. What is this college's graduation rate? Graduation rates are difficult to calculate because not every student enrolls in classes for the same number of credits, participates in the same on- and off-campus opportunities (like study abroad and athletics), or has the same academic or financial background. You need to know how many students who matriculated as first-time freshmen graduate within four, five, and six years. Tell the college what you want to study, the programs in which you'll want to participate, and how many credits you'd like to take each year. Then you'll get an idea of how many semesters it will take to earn your degree.

9. How large is this college's endowment? Individuals, families, foundations, and corporations give to colleges and universities for a variety of reasons, but a large endowment doesn't mean a college can afford to provide every student with scholarships and other support during their four (or more) years of undergraduate study. There are lots of issues to review here. Here are a few general facts and questions to help shape what you might ask the faculty of the department or program in which you're interested.

10. How many students are accepted into graduate school? Don't just jot down the percentage—ask the tough questions. If you plan on attending graduate school, ask for the names of and acceptance rates at the universities most often attended after graduation. Are there any special

arrangements between the college and certain graduate programs?

You're interested in two basic things: scholarships and program support. If scholarship support is available, what are the exact requirements necessary to receive a scholarship? Second, you should always ask what other program support is available.

Ask the faculty whether scholarship support or program funds supporting student educational costs have been affected by economic recession. No matter how big the endowment, if an economic downturn results in a smaller return on a donor's invested gift, find out if scholarships are limited in any way.

The bottom line with endowments is that it isn't just about their published size. All other issues being equal between three top-college choices, you might be more interested in the one that offers the greatest exposure to your major through internships, study abroad, field experiences, and other enhancements that are supported through endowment funds.

You need to learn as much as you can about special scholarships and grants that support undergraduate students. Ask current students who are being supported by scholarships in your prospective major how they applied and what the requirements were when they received support. You can tailor your application essay, your summer leisure, and any related activities and, if you are starting this process early on, some of your high school classes to fit neatly into the requirements for these scholarships.

Searching for the BIG IDEA: Academic Quality and Curriculum Flexibility

Many students enter college simply to broaden their knowledge or to gain a set of skills for a particular career path or graduate school program. Others are looking for an opportunity to test their BIG IDEA. That is, they may have a creative musical streak, an outstanding command of Internet technology, acting skills, a knack for high-level mathematics, or an idea so unique that they need a highly flexible academic program to allow them to pursue all of their passions while incorporating them all into a bachelor's degree. This isn't at all uncommon.

If you're one of these students in pursuit of a college where you can pursue your own BIG IDEA, you need to identify the attributes of a college experience that are important to you and focus on how a college educates you in order to make sure that its teaching methods match how you learn. This is going to be tremendously valuable information when it comes time to put together a winning application to the elite college of your choice.

Search for top-tier colleges that offer all or most of the majors, minors, programs, and services related to your interests. For example, if you are interested in Internet browsers and developing home pages, you should look at colleges that offer computer science, mathematics, technical writing, business and corporate communications, management of information systems, and related fields. Your next step is to explore how each academic department works with other programs across campus and within other disciplines to provide unique experiences for you. It is just as important to determine how your studies, your after-school work, or your hobbies and interests *now* reflect the academic programs that interest you. You're trying to find a match between what you want to do and what a school has to offer.

Let's look at our example of website design. If a college doesn't have a major in Internet technology, is it willing to work up a plan of study with you in which you'll take courses in different departments, ending up with a degree that includes all the skills and internships in the career field in which you're interested? This is a sign of a flexible curriculum.

International Experiences

More high schoolers than ever before want to go to a college that will provide opportunities to study abroad and participate in international programs.

Study-abroad programs allow students to live in other countries while attending classes taught by professors who are in no way affiliated with the students' home institutions. Some programs require fluency in a language, some don't. Some are designed to fully immerse a student into a particular culture, and others may focus on a specific area of academic research.

In an exchange program, students from two or more host institutions swap a semester in each other's colleges in exchange for (usually) an equal number of credits or program requirements. Exchange programs can get complicated. If you're seriously considering applying to a school because of its exchange programs, be certain that the experiences earn credits and that these credits are part of the requirements to graduate within your major, not simply general credits unrecognized as required coursework.

International programs themselves differ greatly between colleges.[1] Most elite colleges have well-developed international programs.

[1] Participating in an international program doesn't always entail studying abroad. International programs usually encompass programming in student life, social events, and cultural events tied to academic programs and usually include language requirements.

Make an appointment with the international programs office staff and faculty. Make sure you address the issues of costs, credits, and progress toward graduation noted above. Speak to students about the requirements for approval of an international experience.

A liberal arts college or university with a strong international or study-abroad program should have a separate office, faculty, and budget, and a cultural and social activities calendar. While you're touring your prospective schools, ask to speak to students who've studied abroad as well as to students from other countries who have spent time on the home school's campus. Try to find out what makes a college's program unique. This will provide you with valuable information when you're putting your application together.

Inside Tip

So you traveled around the world on a Club Med cruise, or maybe you went to Guatemala with your church youth group and participated in two weeks of service work. If you plan to add this to your application, you'll be joining thousands of students who've done the same things. Your goal should be to explain what you learned, not how many miles you traveled. Do you speak a foreign language? Three languages? How can you prove it? Forget the travel magazine approach to the essay question that asks, "How did these experiences change your life?" Write instead about the connections between changing cultural dynamics, world politics, and economic sanctions in neighboring countries. Or has a recent political, religious, or cultural change taken place in any of the countries you've visited? How can you put it into perspective in a way that shows that you not only *want*, but *need* to learn more? Make it clear that you were there to learn—and then relax. If you're able to locate alumni who live in countries you're visiting, find an acceptable way to introduce yourself and carefully try to build an advocate/nominee relationship that results in the alumna sending strong signals to the admissions office that she has found a GREAT student prospect while shopping at the local market.

Making the Most of a Campus Visit

The typical campus visit involves taking a tour with a student guide; sitting in on a class or two; speaking with faculty in your areas of interest; meeting with members of the admissions staff, financial aid officers, and athletic coaches; trying out the local cuisine in the cafeteria (though hopefully, this stop on the tour will be optional), and possibly staying overnight with a student host. To make the most of your visit, here are a few tips on when to visit, what to see, and what to ask while touring. First, arrive early and walk around by yourself. Do people smile and say hello? From your first impression, does it seem as though you'd fit right in?

Next, go to breakfast or lunch by yourself, even if you've been scheduled to have a meal with a student or other college representative. Look around you and listen to the conversations students are having. Do you hear discussions about classes, tests, football games, or sleazy little anecdotes about roommates? Sometimes you can pick up on things that characterize a campus. Do faculty and students eat together, or do professors have their own dining facility? This is another way to find out if professors are accessible beyond regular office hours. While you're there, look closely at the fare the cafeteria offers. Will you be able to stomach at least a year of it?

When you're back out and about, ask your tour guide to take you to specific areas of the campus that interest you. For a personalized tour, ask for a student from your hometown or one in your academic area to guide you. Still curious about the student/faculty ratio? Check out a class in session. You'll see firsthand how many students interact with a faculty member.

Finally, if you really want to see what goes on after a typical day of classes, stay overnight. You'll get much better idea of campus life after your family has left. Spend lots of time looking for practical things such as laundry machines, the fitness center, and relaxation areas (food courts, game rooms, TV lounges, etc.). Are they crowded? What sort of condition are they in?

If possible, schedule your visit to coincide with a popular athletic event or during a play or concert. How well attended are these? Finally, visit a few weeks after the semester starts, or a week or two after midterm exams. Students and faculty are more accessible at these times, and you'll be able to experience the campus community on a routine day.

Defining Faculty-Student Interaction

During many college tours and interviews, prospective students ask, "Are faculty members accessible?" Expect the same answer at every college you explore: a resounding "Yes!" Prepare yourself to dig deeper into this issue because these are the professors you will be working with for four years.

If you can, walk through faculty offices. Take note of two things: first, check out the office hours posted on the faculty doors. Are the hours reasonable enough to work with the schedules of the students in his or her classes? Second, are students consulting with faculty as you pass by, and if so, are many students waiting outside for their turn? If a bunch of students are waiting, is this a good thing or a bad thing? It can mean that a) the professor has very restrictive office hours that everyone tries to bunch up on or b) the students love the professor or desire her guidance so much that she's always stampeded during office hours.

Colleges and Networking: Is it Really Who You Know?

It's important to understand that it's what you know and learn, as well as who you know, that combine to help you promote your skills, knowledge, and professional attitude to companies. No college or university can guarantee all students jobs in fields of their choice directly after graduation. But they can put resources at your fingertips that can help you.

During your visits to colleges, ask to see the career centers. You should find the usual collection of job postings or internships currently available to graduates, workshops on resume writing, and books and brochures of job opportunities in fields that interest you.

You should also ask if you can have a copy of the latest alumni directory. Many colleges list by the alumni's career type and location. You may have to pay a small fee for the book. If the career center refuses, that's okay. It's trying to protect the privacy of its alumni. Instead, ask for the names of five or ten alumni in different career fields that interest you and in different age brackets who would be willing to accept a call from a prospective student.

Remember, it's not just what you've learned in a college, but the successes of those who graduated before you that helps you decide if you are making the right choices. And believe us, a lot of successful people graduated from elite colleges. The more contact you make with alumni, the better off you'll be as you develop your network of who you know when you are ready to apply for admission and, ultimately, when you interview for your first job.

Having read this chapter, you should be forming ideas about what's most important to you in terms of what you want to learn, how you learn, and what kind of experiences and people you want to be exposed to while enjoying your undergraduate years.

Now it's time to translate all of these ideas into a compelling, Ivy-caliber application.

Chapter 7

Applications:
The Story of You

Aldous Huxley once said that it's just as hard to write a bad novel as it is to write a good one. Both require a lot of work, and the writer has no guarantee that either is going to be a critical success once it goes to the reviewers. Wise writers know that a successful novel must first be a well-told, good story. But there's also a human factor, an element of uncertainty, involved: different critics will love or hate a book for personal reasons particular to each of them. It's not going to be a winner with them all, but if it has meaning for a critic at an internal level (and the story's good and well-told), you can bet she'll write a stellar review of it. If one writes a bad novel, though, no matter how much he worked on it, he doesn't have much to look forward to from his critics.

Think of completing your elite college applications as writing a novel. At certain points in the process you're going to feel like you're writing a book, anyway. And think of the admissions officer at the elite college of your choice as your critic—your toughest critic. She's first going to be looking for a well-told, good story.

And just what is that? As far as what well-told means, you'll get some specific tips in Chapter 8 about writing style. So let's talk about story. A good story is engaging. It has characters that are complex and passionate, who don't just dream, but do. Sometimes they fail, sometimes they succeed, but they are always doing. Nobody wants to read about a character that sits around all day with his head in the clouds. A good story has a plot—a series of happenings—that is consistent and leads to a convincing conclusion.

You're the main character in the story of your application. When completing it, your primary goal is to reveal yourself as an interesting character: someone who is passionate, yet not obsessive; someone who dreams, but also, and more importantly, someone who strives to achieve his or her dreams consistently.

Your toughest critic, the admissions officer, is going to look for attributes of your story's main character that are important to her college at an internal level. If you've followed our advice from Chapter 6, you can eliminate the human factor, or at least diminish it, because you should now know what's internally important at your top-choice college. If the story you tell through your essays, activities, and recommendations convinces the admissions committee that your passion will contribute to the campus community, and you have the grades and test scores of a champion besides, you'll no doubt get the fat envelope.

All of this will require some reflection and planning. It also means taking time to draw connections between your goals and the attributes of that college that will help you fulfill those goals. It's not going to be the easiest thing you've ever done, but if you follow our advice, it could turn out to be interesting and rewarding.

Okay then. Take a deep breath and fire up your computer and your imagination. If you don't have a computer, get one (we trust you have an imagination).

Read Any Good Books Lately?

Today the official paper version of an ultra-selective school is about as thick as the telephone book of a small town. That means there's going to be a lot of documents you'll have to keep in order. "Which," you may be thinking, "is why I prefer to apply online." And you're right. Use the *APPLY!* system on www.review.com. It's free, populates each application with answers from the last one you fill out, allows you to sort your applications by priority, and keeps you up-to-date on deadlines. When you're done with an application, you can print out a sharp-looking hard copy and mail it in the old-fashioned way or, with many colleges, you can electronically submit your applications.

Inventory Control

Not all applications will require exactly the same documents from you, but the most extensive will want what's outlined below.

Part 1: The Easy Part

You can spell your name, and know your address, social security number, and basic information about your family. Fill out this form as soon as you get it, indicating whether you're applying early decision, early application, or regular decision (ED, EA, or RD), and return it. The college now has a file open on you. Step one is done.

Part 2 : The Not-So-Easy Part

Now it gets serious. Part 2 zeroes in on your specifics. Required information includes your transcript, recommending teachers' names, major academic honors, AP courses taken, AP test scores, college courses, and SAT scores (I and II). You'll also need to list your interests and school-year activities, summer-activity history, and after-school jobs. You might also run into a little section that asks you a series of seemingly innocuous questions, like what your favorite time of day is and which movie is your favorite.

All of this might seem straightforward, but it's not, and you have to pay close attention to your answers, what activities you choose to include, and how you present them. Keep in mind that the nation's best colleges aren't looking for well-rounded students; they're trying to build a well-rounded student body. They want a campus with a variety of passionate people, not one full of kids with a bunch of interests. (Passion is boundless enthusiasm; interest is just curiosity.) These extracurricular/work/summer activities forms are where you begin to document your passion. And you can't have twelve passions. You may have two, like the young man whose application we provide below, but certainly not more than that.

Remember how your application as a whole is the story of you. You, as the applicant, are mounting an argument through each part of it, not only in the formal essays. You therefore want your activities and awards to act as proof of your passion. If your passion is poetry, this is where it needs to show up first, in the form of prizes you've won in contests, workshops you've taken over the summer, contributions you've made to any literary publications, and the college poetry class you're taking at night right now. This is also where you list any alumni you know. Don't leave anyone out.

Of course, there are also the two teacher recommendation forms, the secondary school report, and the counselor recommendation form. You don't complete these yourself, but you do have to manage them.

Part 3: Essays—Who You Are Is What You Should Write

Question:
What's the biggest reason why quality applicants get rejected from elite colleges?

Answer:
Their inability to put together a convincing written argument.

How You Should Write
Voice is an ability to make your reader hear you talking through your written words. That's your essay challenge. The best resource to help you find your own voice is *The Elements of Style*, by William Strunk Jr. and E.B. White. Read it thoroughly. If you do not own a copy of this book, get one immediately.

What You Should Write

Admissions committees don't want to hear about your summer vacation in Europe or your plan to end world hunger. In fact, they'd rather read your observations about how often cars run yellow lights at the intersection near your home. The reason is that writing about that intersection can tell more about who you are and how you think than an essay about the needs of the entire world. As you read the real-life essays in this chapter, pay attention to how the writer reveals his attitudes, preferences, strengths, and weaknesses in everyday situations. His life is no more exciting or glamorous than yours.

The most thorough applications will require a bevy of essays, including: (1) three brief essays on general topics, (2) three program-specific essays (if you are applying to a particular major or program), (3) a Big Essay, (4) an anything else essay, and (5) three optional update essays.

Special Forms

Most selective colleges provide applicants with some sort of optional reference form, which gives you an excellent opportunity to have someone who knows you well write a recommendation for you. Just be aware that the more selective the school, the less optional the form. So take advantage of it. Your referrer should be a quality writer. The more insight this person can provide regarding who you are the better, but be sure that what any reference says is consistent with the rest of your application.

Inside Tip: Recommendations

Take your recommendations seriously. Don't pick someone as a referrer just because you think he is a great teacher. Pick someone who you know writes well. You should generally avoid having math and science teachers write recs for you. The best recommendations usually come from English and social studies teachers. Whoever writes a recommendation for you, though, should know you well and have reasons to speak highly of you. Admission committees appreciate specific anecdotes about you in recommendations.

The biggest red flag admissions committees see in essays and recommendations is inconsistency. How do admissions officers spot inconsistencies in personal recommendations? Here are two examples:

- Say Sue's English teacher in twelfth grade writes, "Sue is among the top three students I have had the pleasure of teaching in my 27 years in the classroom. She consistently proves her understanding and command of tense, verse, and in-depth analysis of the classics, her original writings, and those of her classmates. She has served as a writing tutor and mentor to underclass students for the past three years." What do the members of the the admissions committe do? They immediately take out the transcript, the essay, and anything else they can get their hands on to check for consistency. If they find that her grades have not been consistent in required English classes, electives, and even AP classes, their suspicions rise. If the essay proves that Sue's writing ability is not what the teacher says it is, their suspicion turns into a hunt for the truth. Finally, Sue must list her tutoring activities somewhere on the application. This should match what the teacher stated in terms of duration, and it is helpful to have the name of the faculty or staff who directs the tutors. They'll call if something doesn't look right, or if any of the issues listed above raise a question.

- Say Rafael's after-school employer writes: "Rafael has worked part-time after school as a technical writer for my company for the past two years. He is never late and does not stop until he finds a solution to the problem or challenge he has been given. His determination to finish the job has been a hallmark of his performance for the past two years." Many admissions officers will look at the after-school activities in which a student has been involved. If they find that Rafael has spent only six months each in five different school activities, and never more than one year in any sport, club, or other activity, they'll question the word "determination" and wonder if Rafael is simply testing everything and committing to nothing. That's fine during the first semester or two at college, but then a student must commit and be consistent, which leads to persistence, which results in an on-time graduation.

Give a copy of everything you've already submitted (or are planning to submit) about your academics, activities, and work to each of your referrers before they write your recommendation. This minimizes the chance that they'll inadvertantly write something that hurts your application. Make sure that your referrers know what your passion is, if they don't already. Recommendations are an integral part of the story of you; they're just being told by someone else. If an admissions officer reads about your passion in a recommendation and it reinforces all that you've written about yourself and shown through your high school activities, your chances of acceptance improve.

Stanford University, known as "The Farm," is one of the most architecturally unique colleges in the United States. Stanford's Class of 2005 is the most diverse in the school's history, with 49.9 percent of admitted students representing minority groups. Popular majors include engineering, biology, economics, history, political science, English, and psychology. Ninety-three percent of those enrolling as freshmen graduate within five years.

The Real Thing

The sample below comes from the application of a young man who applied and was accepted to one of the most selective undergraduate engineering programs in the country. For reasons of privacy, we have given him the fictitious name of "Graham." He's the same kid we mentioned in Chapter 3.

The Cover Letter

Lots of people wonder why you would ever need a cover letter for a college application. The letter does three things.

1. It shows that the applicant has his act together. Notice that Graham has accounted for all the elements of his application package. He tells Stanford what's included and what to expect from others who are sending in supporting materials.

2. It justifies the applicant's position. Graham tells it like it is: "Stanford is my clear, first-choice school." That statement is music to the admissions committee's ears. It's nice to know where an applicant's heart lies.

3. It adds a touch of humor. The effective use of humor is probably the most misunderstood and underused element in college applications. Graham's comment about ditching the typewriter is a nice touch.

Here's the cover letter.

Admission Office
Stanford University
520 Lasuen Mall
Old Union 232
Stanford, CA 94305-3005

Ladies and Gentlemen:

This is the completed Part 2 of my application to Stanford University. I have made every effort to be complete and candid, the goal being to present myself as a worthy candidate for next year's freshman class. The following is a list of what I have submitted here and requested from others to complete my admission file:

- Application Part 1 and application fee (mailed separately and at an earlier date)
- Application Part 2 (enclosed here)
- two teacher recommendations (to be mailed separately)
- the Secondary School Report (to be mailed separately)
- the Optional Reference Form

Stanford is my clear, first-choice school. I understand how competitive the admission process is, so I have documented my qualifications as completely as possible. Incidentally, a few portions of the application are hand-printed. We ditched our typewriter when we got a computer. I couldn't format some of the pages for our printer. That's progress, I guess.

Thank you very much for considering my application.

Sincerely,

Graham

The Numbers

Before we get into Graham's essays, it's important to note that he was one of those quality applicants we keep mentioning. What does that mean? Let's look at the hard numbers. Graham scored a combined 1480 on the SAT I (720 Verbal, 760 Math). He took an SAT II test in Chemistry, English Composition, and Math IIC. His scores in each test were, respectively, 680, 720, and 680. He was valedictorian of a class of 600, with a final GPA over 100%. He had taken four Advanced Placement tests: Calculus AB, Computer Science A, German, and Physics. He scored a 5 on all of them except German, on which he scored a 4. He ended up being a National Merit Finalist. These are numbers that elite college admission committees like to see, so Graham was already in good shape before they read these very well-written essays.

Interests and Activities

For his statement on interests and activities, Graham attached a separate summary, since the two inches of space allowed on the application page could hardly contain a comprehensive look at his activities. You should pay attention to three things. First, most of what he lists bridges his high school years. This is the first piece of evidence that Graham has dedication and consistency. Second, listing his achievements with computers, math, and science supports what he calls in his essays his "passion for engineering sciences," while the rest shows that he's not completely obsessed with them. Third, his self-taught guitar lessons and his subsequent time spent writing and recording songs shows that he has initiative, that if he wants to learn something, he will find a way to do it, even if it means teaching himself. An interesting character is already starting to shape up.

Summary of Academic Awards, Achievements, and Activities for Graham

Saxophone study: marching band, concert band, and jazz ensembles (9th through 12th grades)

Self-taught guitar studies: acoustic/electric pop and classical (9th grade to present)

Played varsity tennis (singles and doubles) (9th through 12th grades)

Made state finals of Odyssey of the Mind competition (10th grade)

Won Honorable Mention, Martin Luther King Jr. Essay Contest sponsored by The Pennsylvania State University (10th grade)

Selected as member, German Honor Society (10th through 12th grades)

Made state finals, American Association of Teachers of German Competition (11th grade)

Selected as candidate for Cornell University computer research project (10th grade)

Named National Merit Scholarship Semifinalist (Finalist pending) (12th grade)

Attended the Pennsylvania Governor's School for the Sciences at Carnegie Mellon University, Pittsburgh, PA (summer between 11th and 12th grade)

Elected president, High School Computer Club (11th grade)

Elected vice president, National Honor Society, school chapter (12th grade)

Won the Rensselaer Medal as top junior in mathematics and science (11th grade)

Participated in Pennsylvania Math League competitions, placing in the top ten six out of eight times (10th and 11th grades)

Wrote, played, and recorded own compositions for voice and guitar (solo and group) (9th through 12th grades). 15–20 hours/week

Attended summer school: summers following 10th and 11th grades

Summary:

Tutor classmates and friends in all levels of math, science, and German; give private guitar lessons (9th grade to present). 2-4 hours/week.

Work for disabled grandmother doing lawn care, winter and summer house preparations, and general chores (8th grade to present). 2-6 hours/week.

Help in father's business doing computer graphics, database maintenance, and advertising work (10th grade to present). 1-3 hours/ week.

Here's his statement addressing summer work and activities (notice that this is more than just a casual listing):

The past two summers were a mixture of learning, work, and relaxation. In both, I took summer school classes to make room in my fall schedule for more advanced courses. My usual summer work continued: working for my disabled grandmother, doing neighborhood yard work, and giving guitar lessons (when not improving my own skills on that instrument). The bulk of last summer was occupied by the Pennsylvania Governor's School for the Sciences at Carnegie Mellon University. My relaxation: playing guitar and reading.

The Seemingly Unimportant Questions

Graham listed his favorite in each category.

Book: 1984 by George Orwell

Keepsake: Photo of me with my PA Governor's School friends

Recording: Pink Floyd's "Wish You Were Here"

Time of the day: Early evening (6:00 p.m.–8:00 p.m.)

Activity: Playing the guitar

Academic subject: Physics

Movie: Monty Python and the Quest for the Holy Grail

Expression: "Go figure!"

Section of newspaper: Classifieds

Source of news: Headline News

Quotation: "The question, O me! so sad, recurring—What good amid these, O me, O life?/That you are here—that life exists and identity,/ That the powerful play goes on, and you may contribute a verse." Walt Whitman, *O Me! O Life! —Leaves of Grass*

Three Questions

1. If you were given the opportunity to spend one year in service on behalf of others, which area would you choose? Briefly explain why.

Since I love to teach, tutoring my fellow students would be a great way to spend a year. I have significant experience tutoring; I've been part of my school's peer tutoring group for the past three years. My specialties include such diverse areas as German, calculus, history, and physics. In addition to tutoring these purely academic subjects, I also give several of my friends guitar lessons. Helping others to learn is an excellent way for me to improve my own learning skills. When I work with a fellow student or friend, I get to experiment with various teaching methods. Their varied learning preferences make me adapt my approach for the best results. Some of my most satisfying moments have come from tutoring experiences—when I get to see the look of understanding in their eyes, hear that tone of confidence in their voices, or learn of their high test grades or reports well received. The satisfaction for me is meeting the challenge of communicating a broad range of new concepts and ideas to people I know and respect.

2. Of all the things you hope or expect to gain from your college experience, which two or three would you place at the top of your list if you had to make up such a list today? (Be as specific or as general as you'd like.)

My hometown is homogenous. There is very little diversity here. Most people are white, politically conservative, lower- to upper-middle class working people. This, I have to admit, has made me somewhat narrow-minded on certain issues. High on my list of college expectations is the hope for a truly life-changing experience with a thoroughly diverse student body. I want my limited viewpoint of the world changed from tunnel vision to virtual reality. I want to find out who I really am, what I really love. I want a more diverse range of experiences.

I also expect the college I attend to be able to deliver a first-class program that will allow me to indulge my two divergent passions: literature and engineering. One of the things I've learned about myself is that the scales of my interests seem to be balanced. I love science and math, but I also love words and ideas. The closest I've ever come to an ideal learning experience came this past summer at the Pennsylvania Governor's School for the Science, which I attended at Carnegie Mellon University. The course that proved so stimulating was *Art and Science*, which explored the important contributions each discipline has made to the other. Literature and engineering may seem unrelated, but I want to make an in-depth study of both in college.

3. What kind of person would you consider an ideal roommate for your freshman year in college?

Quirky or idiosyncratic people don't bother me. I won't say that my friends here at home are a little odd, but I have learned to deal with some excesses of weirdness in others. Accordingly, I would hope to have a roommate who is his own, unique person, with a good sense of humor.

It would also be nice if he comes from a completely different background than I do, complete with an inventory of different ideas. In other words, I don't want to room with a nice, safe, carbon copy of myself just to make things easy. If my roommate stays out later or gets up earlier than I do, so be it. But I hope at least he would be tolerant in the same ways to me. I could have fun with a roommate like this. We could both learn from our differences.

Incidentally, I noticed that you dropped your little note on this question from last year's application about assigning roommates of the same sex for the foreseeable future. I'm assuming that's still your policy. If not, though, the above comments still apply.

The Program-Specific Essays

Graham applied specifically to Stanford's engineering program and had to answer these questions.

1. Why are you interested in studying engineering?

Engineering combines the theory and application of math and physics, the two technical areas in which I have the most ability and interest. Engineering, therefore, provides a forum for my science and math skills that could result in a development that could change the world in some practical way. To paraphrase Walt Whitman, the verse I might contribute could affect the outcome of the play.

Projects I've worked on in AP Physics and, most notably, the course *Concepts of Modern Physics* at the Pennsylvania Governor's School for the Sciences have drawn me to engineering. Seemingly simple challenges like designing a shock mitigation device to protect an egg dropped from 15 meters, a basswood bridge designed to bear heavy loads, or a mousetrap-powered vehicle have fascinated me and satisfied my innate desire to solve practical problems creatively.

2. Briefly describe any particular experiences you have had that are related to engineering or that led you to have an interest in one or another field of engineering.

The most significant event that has led me to engineering has been my involvement with the Pennsylvania Governor's School for the Sciences (PGSS), which I attended this past summer at Carnegie Mellon University. I had full-blown college courses in discrete mathematics, computer science, molecular biology, the philosophy of science, chemistry, physics, art and science, and a team project. Our team project—The Establishment and Analysis of Chaos in a Forced Duffing Oscillator—was in physics and examined the order present in seemingly chaotic patterns. I also performed special studies of mechanical and electrical-circuit resonance. For five intensive weeks we studied, wrote, analyzed, reported, learned, and laughed. I loved it.

3. How do you think the program in engineering at Stanford might suit your particular interests?

You asked me elsewhere in this application what I expect to gain from my college experience. I said I wanted a first-class program that allowed me to indulge my passions for engineering sciences and literature. That's exactly how I see Stanford Engineering suiting my interests. It's the balance of the program I like. The humanities and social science requirements comprise almost 20% of the B.S.E. program. I truly want to pursue engineering in college; I wouldn't be offended, though, if my School of Engineering associates thought of me as a poet.

Another factor has to be Stanford's faculty and physical resources. My parents and I took an unofficial tour of the engineering facilities on a sunny Saturday morning last August. The buildings were empty and quiet, which gave me the chance to peer unnoticed through lab door windows and into lecture rooms and faculty offices. The overwhelming impression was that of being somewhere important, where things of consequence happen. Call it a spirit of greatness. Whatever it is, it kept prompting me during our long drive home. My needs would be met here.

The Main Essay

> In the space below, tell one story about yourself that would best provide us, either directly or indirectly, with an insight into the kind of person you are. For example, the story can simply relate a personal experience, or a humorous anecdote; it can tell about an especially significant academic encounter or about an unusual test of character. The possibilities are unlimited (well, almost so). You choose. Just relax and write it. (Remember, Lincoln's "Gettysburg Address" was only 272 words.)

Once upon a time, I thought I knew it all. Now, though, I realize there's a universe of knowledge yet to obtain. When did I come to this revelation? Well, it wasn't some brilliant epiphany flashing before my eyes in the shower one morning. It was, rather, a slow, humbling process, at once frustrating and necessary. So there I was, cruising along, a kind of God's Gift to Academia. Then came the speed bump known as the Pennsylvania Governor's School for the Sciences (PGSS): five weeks of mind-crushing science studies at Carnegie Mellon University. The strange part? I loved it.

Getting into PGSS is almost as hard as going through it. Would it be an intellectual heaven or an academic hell? I had no idea what to expect as my parents and I headed out that Sunday morning in late June. "Farewell friends. Farewell guitar. Farewell summer," I mourned as the tar strips clicked off under our Civic's tires. "Camp Saskatchewa, here I come." Funny thing, though. From my first moment there, I knew this was not summer camp. The intellectual brilliance fairly crackled in the air, arcing over the very dorm where we were to live. And my bags weren't even unpacked.

By Day Two, I was plunged into an academic program the intensity of which I'd never known: lectures for breakfast and lunch, from 8:00 a.m. to 2:00 p.m., followed by three hours of lab time or team project work. The team project—the hub of PGSS—lasted a full five weeks and culminated in a formal research report and a presentation to the entire faculty and student body. It was a turning point, pushing me to (and beyond) the limits of what I thought my brain could accommodate. I'm especially motivated by physics, so I chose that discipline for my project area. Besides, the topics just seemed more valuable and unique.

We called ourselves Team Chaos: Ellen, Oren, Tom, and Graham. The focus of the project was chaos and chaotic motion. I'm no stranger to chaos, a fact to which my bedroom closet bears witness. I pegged Ellen, a tall blonde, immediately; she was the workaholic, the die-hard, the one who went to the library that first night and brought back six books on the study of chaos. Ellen's antithesis was Oren, a brilliant, albeit laid-back, sandal-wearing lover of punk rock. As I contrasted Ellen and Oren, visions of Team Conflict danced in my head. Tom, like me, lay somewhere between the two poles of what Ellen and Oren represented. That comforted me for the moment.

We got the research done. Sometimes it was messy (yes, even chaotic) and there were more than a few squabbles about who was going to work on what. But the work got done. Tom and I would watch Ellen yell at Oren who would often fall asleep which would in turn inspire Ellen to start tearing at her hair. The circle of conflict was really quite amazing. As the tensions and fatigue escalated sharply the week before our report was due, I wondered what I had gotten myself into. I would fall exhausted into my bed (usually around 4:00 a.m.) and dream of sleeping until noon. I would actually dream about sleeping. Another recurring dream was one about living a life that didn't require thinking about chaos. There's a deep psychological principle in there somewhere, but I have no idea what it is.

Then I lost the disk. Why me? In thinking about it now, from a distance, I guess the reason I had control over the disk that contained our report was because I type very quickly. During that frantic final week, we had to collate mountains of research data into a coherent report and presentation. I inherited most of that task. Late nights grew later and later until I was spending all night at the computer center. When did it happen? Who knows? I'd really like to blame it on lack of sleep. I really would. At any rate, I had to search through a garbage can on my hands and knees, foraging for any old work I had tossed. I found a few pages. My sanity was pulled back from the edge of the abyss. And work began again.

There comes a time in everyone's life, I believe, when all seems futile. That time came for me one weary night/morning when I sat dazed and reeling before my computer-cluster monitor. The Chaos report had metamorphosed from mere paper into a Matterhorn of maddening frustration. I felt worthless and weak before its shrouded peak; for the first time in my life, I truly felt at the end of my rope. Then I looked around me for the first time in hours. Ten other numbed and barely functioning PGSS compatriots sat similarly before their screens, contemplating their personal Everests. It wasn't just me, or this project. We were all in this together.

Humility does wonders for one's focus. The strength came from somewhere to finish our report that night, all thirty pages. The research aspect of our project was intriguing, but the real learning came from the process. I was cleansed by the fire of dozens of sleepless nights. I found out how far I could push myself and that the seemingly impossible task can be achieved. Yes, once I thought I knew it all, but I emerged from that refining fire a different person, one who humbly realizes there is still much to learn, not only about science but also about life.

Optional Anything Else You'd Like to Tell Us Essay

This is the form to use if there's anything else you'd like to tell us that we haven't asked you about on the application. If you believe that there is some fact, experience, talent, thought, or whatever which just didn't seem to fit into our application but which you'd like us to take into consideration, let us know about it here.

College applications are serious business. If I can leave you with one impression to remember me by, however, I want it to be of my positive sense of humor, my spirited joy for learning. Anecdotes are usually good for making one's point. Here are a few to make mine.

The assignment for History class was straightforward; make a team presentation satirizing television news coverage. We grabbed a camcorder and on a hot, humid Saturday climbed the rocks to the top of a nearby cliff, carefully dragging what we planned to throw from its peak: the limp, lifeless form of a man. With sweat blurring our vision, we squinted to survey the target below—a church parking lot. After one last walkthrough, we rolled the tape and heaved our newsmaker over the edge.

Granted, our star was only a newspaper-stuffed pair of jeans and shirt with a Ronald Reagan-mask head. But when the final, edited footage (complete with voice-overs and cutaways to our reporter) played for our class, they loved it. I co-wrote, performed in, and produced this *COPS*-like account of a man receiving his due for ignoring that stern warning on a Blockbuster video rental. The sequence was grim testimony to what can happen when you don't rewind. It was our "film at eleven" on *Deadline News*. (I regret we didn't come up with a better name for our newscast but, actually, we did do everything at the last possible moment.)

*****

My philosophy is: Enjoy learning. I didn't fully understand the inspiration behind Chaucer's *Canterbury Tales* until our group sat down to storyboard another of our video visions, the *Tales of Floyd,* an Honors English project. As we scripted the mythical quest of a disparate group of teenagers in pilgrimage to see the band Pink Floyd in concert, I came to understand how Chaucer might have seen the men and women he sent off to Canterbury. Unlike Chaucer's version, though, ours had Jimi Hendrix appearing in the ghostly dream of a burned-out Sixties hippie, commanding him to find the Holy (VW) Beetle. Our little drama certainly wasn't great art, but I'd like to think that the inspiration was similar to Chaucer's.

The core of the *Tales of Floyd* and *Deadline News* team I worked with comes from my elementary school years. In sixth grade, our Odyssey of the Mind team won the Classics Division of the Pennsylvania state competition and we went on to the World Finals at the University of Colorado. I'm still working with some of that team's members. We've always had a good time solving our challenges with creativity and good humor.

Why do I want to you to remember me as a light-hearted learner? Well, the other parts of this application show you, I believe, that I can do serious work. But I want you to know I don't "grind" when I do my academic thing. For me, it's not like giving birth; there's no suffering or pain. I love challenges. As my high school courses have become more demanding, I've enjoyed them all the more. College could be the most fun yet.

Optional Update Form

> This form is provided so that you can file the initial parts of your application in a timely manner (the earlier the better) without being concerned that you won't have an opportunity to catch us up on what you have been doing during the first half of your senior year. Feel free to use all of it or just part of it to let us know how the year is going.
>
> What's new in your life academically?

Some additional information has come out since I mailed in my Early Action application. First, I have received my evaluation from the Pennsylvania Governor's School for the Sciences (PGSS). Particularly satisfying to me is the comment about my work in the physics laboratory. I have also received confirmation of my membership in the National Honor Society.

Our school newspaper, *Mountain Echo,* featured a fellow classmate and me in an interview segment.

What's new in your life in terms of extracurricular interests/activities?

I found a new toy. One of my friends loaned me his multitrack cassette recorder/mixer. It enables me to create my own accompaniments for the songs I've written. The real fun comes in the experimentation. One song I'm working on combines an acoustic guitar foundation track playing a passacaglia bass figure overlaid with the melody and chords on another track. My vocals are mixed in with the guitar tracks. The whole thing has a kind of gentle other-worldliness about it. I'm not ready to unleash *Graham Unplugged* yet, but I'm close. I'm negotiating with my parents about getting my own recorder for Christmas. Ideally, I'd like to record an album of my own songs, adding sounds from my saxophone and electronic keyboard.

Anything else?

Not at the moment.

Graham also had to manage three referrers (two of his teachers and his father, who completed Graham's optional reference form). He couldn't write these himself, obviously, but he had to stay on top of his referrers to make sure that they sent the admissions committee their letters on time. Teachers already have to put up with a lot from teenagers, so it's best to handle this managing process delicately. Remember that teachers are very busy people with lives of their own and that they'll find it annoying if you think that writing your recommendation is the sole reason they wake up in the morning. We can't tell you how to be diplomatic (although the ability to read people will be an invaluable tool in college), but we can tell you that it's not just important, but imperative that you get all teacher reference forms for Ivy League and elite colleges to your teachers as soon as possible. When's that? The day you seriously decide to apply.

Linda Cicero-Stanford News Service

Stanford University, located in Stanford, California, was founded in 1885 by Leland and Jane Stanford and opened for business in 1891. Perennially among America's most selective universities, Stanford's overall acceptance rate for the Class of 2005 was 12.7%. One recent incoming first-year class of the school's 6,600 undergraduates (almost equally men and women) claims the following credentials: 87% in the top 10% of their high school classes, almost 50% with straight-A grades, and 99.8% with a 3.0 or higher GPA.

Cornell, Swarthmore, and Haverford: The Joys of Recycling

Even though he was accepted to Stanford, Graham also applied to Cornell University's School of Engineering, Swarthmore College, and Haverford College. He was accepted by all three. The primary reason he did this was to see the difference in financial aid offers among these top schools.

By the time he finished his application to Stanford, Graham had pretty much written himself out. Luckily, he found he didn't have to do that much more writing for any of these three school's applications. You know, though, that these three schools all require their own serious essays from applicants. How did Graham get away with having to write very little extra? Since he had written so much for his Stanford application, all he did was adapt what he'd written to sufficiently answer all these other school's essay questions.

Put your very best efforts into the most difficult application among your college choices. The others should flow out of the strength of that first one. Think about it in baseball terms: you only need to hit one home run to score four runs. Don't try to force-fit an obviously mismatched essay from one application into another just because you're committed to recycling, though. It will stick out and you'll pay the price for your laziness.

Inside Tip: Divergence and Balance

Graham's application, taken as a whole, describes what admissions officers consider the perfect student. Look at his response to the second of the three questions (page 99): "I also expect the college I attend to be able to deliver a first-class program that will allow me to indulge my two divergent passions: literature and engineering." Let's call this a marker in Graham's total application. Admissions committees look for this marker, and when it is consistently presented to them and justified throughout the applicant's academic record, cocurricular interests, and personal life, they know they have an exceptional candidate. Here's what an admissions committee would see in this application, and how they would find similar markers consistent in his application.

- "I also expect the college I attend to be able to deliver..." Sounds ballsy at first—an 18-year-old expecting Stanford to be able to deliver something, as if his requirements aren't met, he's taking his business elsewhere. In reality, the thousands of applicants who were denied from Stanford hoped they would just get their credentials considered. Graham expects Stanford to "deliver," or else what? It doesn't matter. This is David looking up at Goliath and imagining that the situation is turned around, as if Goliath is one among many that David could choose to tangle with. It's up to Goliath to prove to David that he has what it takes, not the other way around. Why is this important? It tells the admissions officers that Graham knows he's the underdog, but if he's accepted, he'll run with the ball, lead in classroom discussions, press the faculty for answers, question everything, and in general get to know everything Stanford offers so his time and money is well spent there. He knows himself and, even at a young age, self-assurance is a superb trait if it's balanced with other characteristics.

- "...my two divergent passions: literature and engineering." An admissions committee will look for evidence that he feeds this passion regularly in his classwork, extracurricular activities, reading in and out of the classroom, and with any of his hobbies. They see references to literature throughout his application, whether it be Chaucer's Canterbury Tales, his favorite book, 1984 by George Orwell, or his favorite quote from Walt Whitman. They find practical and theoretical exposure to science and engineering everywhere, like the Governor's School sessions at Carnegie Mellon. Particularly impressive is the naming of a specific team research project by name: "The Establishment and Analysis of Chaos in a Forced Duffing Oscillator." Know what that is? Even if you don't know, it's impressive, right? It shows that Graham is already researching at a level normally found in upper-level undergraduate classes (or even graduate school). He's doing his passion.

- "Balance." Graham uses this term throughout his application. Why is balance so important? Some of the world's most brilliant people balance their work with something that seems absolutely opposite from it. All work and no play makes Jack a dull boy, right? Einstein's sense of humor and love of music, for example, was evident throughout his life. While Graham could have been a 100% bookworm, our guess is that it was his balance between academics and his leisure and his love of learning that stood out for the Stanford admissions committee. What Graham may not have realized was how his passions, although seemingly far apart, defined him as a student who really had his act together.

- Finally, Graham mentioned volunteer service. While many students seem to list every task performed during a Habitat for Humanity project, often stretching a single instance into a lifetime pattern of service to others, or are clearly doing it because they know it's being examined, Graham gave of his time and himself for a family member in need.

Extras

Many students wonder whether they should ever send something extra—something an application does not specifically ask for—to an admissions committee. This is a tough one, as it could both help and harm you, and we'll leave it to your best judgment.

If you choose to send something extra, though, you should be absolutely sure that whatever it is tells an admissions committee something about you and your passion that you couldn't have communicated through your application. If your passion is software, and you just finished an interactive video game that really showcases your skills, by all means send it. The same goes for more mundane things like letters of recommendation. One extra letter written by someone who knows and admires you and your passion can help. Sending two extra things to an admissions committee might hurt you, and sending three definitely will. Err on the side of economy. Admissions officers are busy, underpaid people whose desks are cluttered enough.

Chapter 8

Essays We Have Known Elsewhere

To give you some more perspective on application essays, we're going to discuss some essays of successful elite college applicants. We'll make some background comments about the writers (some names have been changed for privacy), comment on their essay(s), and throw in some tips about the essay process as a whole. Hopefully, you'll come away with some ideas of what, or who, you want to write about in your own application essays.

One thing before we continue: every time a new book comes out on college applications and the essays they require, admissions officers start joking about what theme is going to dominate the pile of essays they have to face. One year, one of these books featured this kid's highly successful essay describing his grandfather's death. Guess what that year's theme was? Yep, death and dying. It was a pretty depressing year for admissions committees. People were dropping like flies. Anybody who wrote about somebody kicking the bucket, no matter how poignant a story it was, didn't stand out. And the key to getting admitted is to stand out. So don't write essays like the ones below. They're good, but they aren't yours. Your application is your story. These are just examples of how successful applicants wrote theirs.

Penn, Early Decision

Julie Chow is an Asian American first-year student at the University of Pennsylvania. She moved to America as a very young girl, learned English, and attended a competitive public high school in the Southwest.

Here is one of Julie's application essays for Penn. She chose to accent her heritage and good sense of humor in a statement that reflects her respect of family, cultural tradition, and some of those awkward moments from her youth that she'd rather forget. As you read, you can almost picture Julie in the midst of the scenes she describes. That's her voice, and it's why this is quality writing.

Banana Girl

I reached for a fish ball (my favorite), wedging the chopsticks tightly between my fingers. I felt a little clumsy leaning toward that center dish. The dinner wasn't all that formal, but I was trying to make a good impression. Then suddenly, my hand-eye coordination failed.

Ten pairs of eyeballs watched in horror as my precious little fish ball squirted out the side of my sticks and bounced onto the table. In what seemed like one of those slow-motion dream sequences from the movies, I watched the little sphere leave a telltale trail of sauce as it rolled determinedly toward the table's edge. I tried to be cool. "No big deal," I thought, as I quietly tried to scoop it with my chopsticks. When that failed, I tried a stab, which only pushed it farther away.

I quickly tried to cover my embarrassment by plastering a bright smile on my ever-reddening face. My father, who was witnessing this dining mini-drama, deftly secured the little ball and, with skill and grace, deposited it into my bowl. "Hmm," he muttered with a sigh, "Can't even use chopsticks." A woman next to him joked, "A Chinese girl who can't use chopsticks?!" Other guests bit their lips, trying to suppress their laughter. As I pondered this unlikely scene, I couldn't fault their amusement. After all, it was remarkable how un-Chinese I had become.

My friends call me "Banana Girl": yellow skin on the outside and white on the inside. At times, I think I'm not Asian anymore, such as during the fish-ball incident. A while ago, my mother sagely predicted that it wouldn't be long before hamburgers and pizza would be a big part of my diet (they already represent two of my four daily food groups). "No problem for me," I said. I was okay with that. "Nothing wrong with being 'Americanized'," I thought. What people don't understand is that, although I am well adapted to America's culture, I still greatly respect Chinese traditions.

When my great-grandmother died this past summer, we couldn't attend her funeral due to financial difficulties. Her death was unexpectedly sudden. So, out of respect for her and our Chinese heritage, we created our own funeral ceremony at home. My mother and I went to our local Chinese market and bought a number of items made of paper (aprons, plates, and other household goods). We even got some Chinese paper money. Then my mother got out her large cooking pot and we went into the back yard and put all the paper items (even the money) into the pot and began burning them.

Chinese, especially the Cantonese people, believe that after a person dies, they move on to another life where they still need practical things like money and clothes. The only way the dead can receive these items is if their relatives gather and burn them, sending them into the air as smoke. After we completed the ceremonial burning, we prepared a feast in remembrance of my great-grandmother. This meal is a kind of symbolic "last supper" with the deceased.

I find the tradition both elegant and comforting. As part of the ceremony, I held up three burning sticks and bowed toward the flaming pot. It was a way to say goodbye and pay respect. Technically, it doesn't make much sense because I bowed to the pot, not to my great-grandmother. I didn't think it was weird at all. I understand and respect that tradition. It is intended to assure that the dead are well provided for. I understand that many traditions aren't logical. It doesn't matter to me, though, because I embrace my Chinese heritage.

I'm pretty sure that I'll probably never master the skill of picking up food with two wooden sticks. In fact, I greatly prefer knives, forks, and spoons. Throughout my cultural transition, though, I've learned that adapting to one culture hasn't "erased" my original identity or my traditional background. I am blessed to have had the advantage of living in and understanding two vastly different cultures. I'm certain that that this diverse perspective will not only help me adapt to the challenges of college life but also bring an element of difference and freshness to my future college friendships. Please remember one thing, though: if fish balls are ever on the dining hall menu, just hand "Banana Girl" a fork!

Look around your everyday life carefully. Scenes like those in "Banana Girl" happen all the time. The key to success is developing the writing skills necessary to make these scenes describe who you are and how you think.

Here's another Penn essay by Julie:

It was past midnight on Christmas day and I was holding a gun. I couldn't concentrate on what I was doing anymore. The clock's second hand ticked louder and my eyelids grew heavier as my contacts rubbed like sandpaper against my bloodshot eyes.

Finally, out of pure frustration, I pulled the trigger. But nothing happened. I was out of glue. Hot-glue guns are like that. I squinted at the floor, littered with tape, glue droppings, wood, broken blades, and so much other stuff that I could hardly find a place to step, let alone find another almost-invisible, clear glue stick. I asked one of my class team members to help. The response was an irritated insult from a weary-eyed creature who once was my friend.

This was but one more chapter in the bitter saga known as "The Rube Goldberg Project." It was the first time that any of us had tried to build a machine. At first I didn't think it would be too hard: just make a contraption of some sort, using as little money as possible, which could move a marble for at least one minute and no more than twenty minutes. Whatever team's machine came closest to either one minute or twenty minutes received the highest grade. It was a deceptively simple challenge.

We didn't waste any time getting started. Lani, a senior and veteran of past Goldbergs, warned, "Don't procrastinate; you'll never finish." Armed with those words of wisdom, we rushed to MJ Designs for our supplies the same day that midterms ended. I even bought paint to decorate our project for extra points. We had no idea the misery that awaited us.

We spent many days endlessly fixing our project and snapping at each other. Finally, one night our friendships fell apart. Jen argued with Karen over the phone for leaving our project to attend a church event. As the bickering and yelling got louder, I just wanted to hide in my closet, but for some reason I didn't let myself collapse into tears. Bending my sore back, I dutifully continued to saw away at a large block of wood. Then, suddenly, the door swung open and Jen ran out of the room, tears streaming down her face. After a long, awkward silence, I explained that it wasn't Karen's fault that she was not going to make it back from church in time. We couldn't let this stop our work. I looked around, picked up the saw, and continued working. Seeing me work, the others started to work too.

I tried to serve as the bond in our group, holding our friendship and our project together. At times, it frustrated me because we buckled so easily, but I was determined that we would succeed and, indeed, we did. We built a "Lost in Space" machine that moved our marble for more than twelve minutes. It involved a staircase, a conveyor belt, and incline planes—a thing of intuitive beauty. Mrs. Killinger, our physics teacher, was so impressed that she awarded us the highest grade in our class.

The grade turned out to be of secondary importance. Mrs. K and our classmates appreciated our hard work, tears, and determination. That's what made it all worthwhile to us. I realized that sometimes, no matter how hopeless things may seem at the moment, as long as I am willing to hang in there for just a little longer, the hard work usually pays off. Tenacity is a virtue. . .which helps when cleaning glue guns too.

Put your best efforts into your lead. You get one chance to draw your readers into your writing. Don't put them to sleep. Also take note of how Julie ties everything up at the end by bringing the focus back to the glue gun. It gives the essay a nice symmetrical structure, kind of an A-B-A form with insights worked into it. Rushing to finish a project is common among almost all high school students, but Julie makes it come alive by paying attention to the details and characters in her story. It sounds authentic.

Julie shows her humor and wit again. The admissions committee will love the focus on team accomplishment, perseverance, and problem solving. As with her last essay, as you read her description of her friendship being challenged, you can practically feel the tears well up in her eyes. The right amount detail gives an essay a genuine feel.

Afternoon Superhero

Meet Jeff Fine from State College, Pennsylvania. Jeff is at Cornell University where he was admitted ED. He may have ended up being one of those many elite-college applicants with terrific stats and stilted essays. Jeff, however, turned out to be a poster kid for those applicants who discover how to write in their own voice after several frustrating false starts.

Here are some of Jeff's winning essays. Can you hear him?

> If you could spend an evening with any fictional character, who would you choose and why?

I won a contest on the radio the other day. The "Hot Five at Five" they call it. I suppose I just got lucky. I asked them what I'd won and they told me I could have either a coupon for an eight-foot hoagie or a one-evening, all-expenses-paid trip to visit the fictional character of my choice. I took the trip. That night I fell asleep trying to decide who I wanted to be with most. You see, I've got a lot of friends in the fiction realm, but I've been kind of strapped financially over the past few years. I haven't been able to visit anyone. Until now.

News of my prize traveled fast. My phone wouldn't stop ringing. The first call was from Dean Moriarty. He's my pal from Jack Kerouac's *On the Road*. He wanted me to meet him in New York and from there, he said, we'd fly to Denver, since the station was footing the bill and all. He said he was tired of making the trip in his old, beat-up jalopy. So much for being on the road. I told him I'd get back to him.

Maggie the Cat called next. She's from Tennessee Williams' *Cat on a Hot Tin Roof*. She said things were finally settling down in her mad family and that she'd love to have me down for Sunday supper. I guess Sunday supper's a big deal in the South. She said Brick wanted to see me too. He's her emotionally unstable, drunkard husband. Anyway, it was great talking to her. While we chatted, though, I got a beep. (How could we live without call waiting?) I told her I'd call her back.

When I clicked over, Doc Brown (from Steven Spielberg's *Back to the Future*) was ranting and raving about me coming to visit him in Hill Valley. He wanted to take me thirty years into the future. Michael J. Fox had given up on him. I told him I'd think about it and be in touch.

More calls followed from old friends like Tom Joad, José Arcadio Buendía, Holden Caulfield, and even Captain Ahab. Then it happened: a collect call from Eternia. After a few seconds of deliberation, I accepted the charges (with parental consent, of course). The familiar voice came across loud and clear. It was He-Man.

I flashed on myself as a six-year-old, plopped in front of our family room TV. I had an action figure in one hand, my magic sword in the other. There was a cape around my neck and a blanket in my lap. That's how it was every weekday afternoon from three-thirty to four, an unwavering routine. Channel Five carried *He-Man* right after *Transformers*. I was the golden-haired warrior's biggest fan, cheering his every move as he fought the evil Skelator on behalf of all Eternians. Eternia's where they all lived.

He-Man told me he needed my help that night. The insidious Skelator was at it again, he said. I couldn't believe it. He-Man, my long lost friend and hero from *Masters of the Universe*, needed *my* help!

Suddenly, I was that little boy again, innocent and infatuated by the ultimate Defender of Good. I knew where my prize would take me: Eternia.

Some people will call me crazy or immature for passing up far more intriguing and captivating characters for He-Man. Granted, he was a trendy, clichéd, short-lived, cartoon superhero, but I didn't think twice.

You see, at the age of six, life's pretty simple. You take things at face value. You admire certain people for their basic qualities. They're your idols because they're good, or generous, or because they help others in need. When you're six, your perception of people is genuine, not colored by the worldly cynicism of adulthood. That's how it should be.

When I was six, I loved He-Man. I didn't care what other people thought of him. He was my hero. I liked him because he was kind, because he provided a moral lesson at the end of every show, and because he fought for what was right. To me, he was The Good Guy. All those other characters who called me are cast as bigger and better by society, more sophisticated, you might say. I don't care. Forget society. I'll pick one of them the next time I win a radio contest. Right now, I'm a little six-year-old boy with an action figure in my hand. He-Man's my main man.

Even if you've never met Jeff Fine, you probably feel as if you know a little something about him after reading this essay. Jeff brings out the fact that he's not only well read, but witty. His choice of He-Man over all the other characters shows that he's a fun kid unconcerned with pretending that he only likes highbrow stuff. Once again, humor doesn't go unnoticed.

Tip: A good lead is invaluable. Nothing puts a reader to sleep faster than an essay that begins: "In thinking about the aspects in which I have been involved for the past ongoing periods of my young life. . ." Can you hear the thud of foreheads hitting the table at colleges nationwide? Grab your readers. Once you grab them, though, don't let them down.

Jeff also discusses growing up and reveals his idealism:"When you're six, your perception of people is genuine, not colored by the worldly cynicism of adulthood. That's how it should be." Chances are you'll never meet the people who read your essays and make the decision about whether or not to let you into their college. So don't be concerned about unmasking yourself. Then again, don't turn your essay into *True Confessions*, filled with all sorts of questionable things about yourself.

Here's another shorter Cornell essay by Jeff:

I just celebrated my 17th birthday; in some ways, I wish it had been my 75th. Please don't misunderstand. By no means do I wish to cut my life short, or sacrifice any of my time on Earth.

There's this thought, though, that bounces around in my head ever so often. It's this spontaneous thing that manifests itself into a burning desire that keeps me up some nights thinking. It comes to me when I realize that there are certain aspects of our society today that pale in comparison to the flavors of past generations. Go figure; maybe I'm just not a 90s kind of guy, but ...

I wish I were Jack Kerouac. For a year or two in the late 50s anyway. You know. Learn for the sake of learning. Write novels based solely on your experiences. Be free and see what's out there, living on apple pie and ice cream. Follow the road less traveled. Ah, the thought. The dream.

I'd like to hitchhike across the country. New York to Berkeley. But with the way things are today, I'd have to worry about the loon who picked me up. He'd probably be some wild-eyed psychopath with a machine gun and a suitcase full of cocaine under a false panel in the back seat and a homemade bomb in the trunk intended to rip off the side of the nearby Federal Building.

What can I say? People have changed. Kerouac hitched a ride with two Midwest farmboys and rode in the bed of their pickup with seven people and a fifth of whiskey. You had pretty good odds back then.

Sometimes it just feels like I've traveled through a generational portal into a society where a lot of things have taken a turn for the worse. I'll take Charlie Parker over Tupac Shakur any day. Give me a million books in a library over all the homepages on the web. I'll take Bogart over Van Damm, Hemingway over Grisham, and Cousey over Rodman. That's just me.

Don't get me wrong. I love my life and the world I live in. Sometimes, though, I just don't get Generation X (or Generation *Next* if you're a Pepsi fan). And when that happens, I simply lie down, close my eyes, and pretend I'm Jack Kerouac. But would I trade the convenience of my word processor for the frustration of an angry typewriter? Get real.

Inside Tip

Don't be afraid to take a stand. Jeff says he's dissatisfied with the status quo and gives the reader some good reasons for his position. His comparisons are reasonable and, therefore, thought provoking. If you feel strongly about something, don't be afraid to say so. Keep the focus personal, though. Don't say something like, "I feel that Iraq is making a big mistake by cutting back oil exports to the West by 10%." They want to know about what *you* believe, not the fact that you read the *Wall Street Journal* and can recycle someone else's economic opinions. That won't buy you much with the admissions committee.

Another Jeff Fine Cornell essay:

Tell us what you'd like to study at Cornell.

It's very possible that I was the first fetus on my block to own a microphone and a tape recorder. Really. Check the sonogram. Don't take that literally, but I'm certain that my future was cast at conception. From day one, I was destined to be a journalist.

They tell me I've never been shy. I guess that's true. As far back as I can remember, I've thrived on interacting with people. I was the kid who always stood up at Cub Scouts to speak to the pack. The others were too embarrassed, but it came naturally to me. Since dealing with people is one of the journalist's key qualities, I already had one foot in the door.

It wasn't until fourth grade, though, that I got my "official" start in journalism. I was asked to participate in this learning enrichment program called Media Magic. The idea was to introduce the world of media to a small group of elementary students. We learned all about newspaper and magazine journalism, and radio and television broadcasting. I loved it. I was a journalist.

During my high school years, *Lion's Digest* (the school paper) has been my passion, my greatest experience, and accomplishment. Never before have I put so much of myself into something. The long hours, tight deadlines, negotiating, stress, and lost weekends were all worth it. Why? For the first time in more than thirty years, the *Digest* won this year's prestigious Keystone Award from the Pennsylvania Scholastic Press Association. I know I was a big part in making that happen. So, I'll get to go up on the stage at the annual conference in Harrisburg and receive our award. I'll glow with pride. I'm a journalist.

Since my freshman year, I have also been "Doctor Fine." Let me explain. I have used that pseudonym every Friday morning on my weekly radio show since the Fall of 1994. I borrowed "Doctor Fine" from my favorite *Three Stooges* episode. It was a good fit; that's who I am. The show opens each week with the Jackson 5 song "I Want You Back." People listen for it. When they hear little Michael belt out those disco lyrics that made him a star, they know it's Friday and they feel good. I've put everything I've got into that show, and when I stroll down the halls at school, friends and strangers alike call me Doctor. I like that. I'm a journalist.

I've barely begun to explore all that the world of communications has to offer. I believe the path to that world begins at Cornell. There I can study everything under the communications umbrella. I can indulge my passion, work for the *Daily Sun*, and all the while receive a world-class education.

A good friend of mine has a T-shirt that reads in bright orange print, "Knowledge is power." I want to be a journalist and I want to study communications. I want to plug into that power. It's my life's calling. I love to learn but I don't want my education to be limited to one umbrella. At Cornell I'll have the opportunity to learn about communications through an ideal curriculum, yet I'll also be able to take the poetry course, the religious studies course, and the business course that will make my education complete and eclectic. I'm a journalist . . . do you read me?

Jeff's recurring theme of "I'm a journalist" works well. It's a kind of self-affirmation. How about that lead and "Check the sonogram"? This is the essay of someone who is confident with his writing style. It's got everything: a good word cadence, sentence structure variety, humor, personal revelations, and creativity. The pun at the end is icing on the cake.

Inside Tip

It's okay to mention a particular award or activity as long as it supports your main point. Jeff's main point, obviously, is that he's a journalist. He presents himself as always having been involved in something to do with communications—even before he was born, which is a great touch. His work with his high school newspaper, the state award, and his radio program are all solid reasons why he should be considered as a serious candidate. Jeff mentions Cornell's school newspaper. That seems like a small thing, but the admissions staff will take note that, by taking the time to investigate the *Sun*, he's done more than many other applicants. All these little pluses add up.

Jeff also took advantage of Cornell's (not-really) optional essay:

Any topic.

Life is all about playing cards. I'm not a gambling man, but that's the way I see it.

Estelle Murphy's deck of cards was old, flimsy, and worn. A few were missing, but she insisted we play anyway. Gin rummy—she said that was her game. As I sat across the table from her at Foxdale Nursing Home that Sunday afternoon, watching her gaze absently at the hand that she was dealt, I could not help but feel sorry for her. Patiently, I waited for her to make a move. She laid down a broken, creased ace of spades and I picked it up. While we sat there, some of the residents of the home wandered aimlessly up and down the halls. Others just sat in their rooms staring out the window. Everyone was trapped— restricted not by the premises, but by the confines of their own minds.

Jimmy Siegel didn't understand blackjack. I was a camp counselor this past summer for a cabin of ten-year-old boys, and every night at about eight o'clock one of them would pull out a brand new deck of playing cards, still stiff from lack of use, and they would sit in a circle on the floor and play blackjack. They gambled with bubble gum and penny candy and they all enjoyed themselves. All of them, that is, except Jimmy. Jimmy was the mentally retarded camper who was unable to catch on right away, so he would sit in his bed and watch. Despite his special needs, Jimmy was one of the most terrific people I've ever known. I guess you could say he was my favorite. I worked with Jimmy and showed him slowly, step-by-step, how the game was played. When it all finally made sense to him, we jumped in with the rest of the guys. Jimmy was dealt a king of spades and an ace of hearts. Blackjack.

A few of my buddies and I get together once a month to play poker. It's become something of a ritual. I have a favorite deck of cards, one that I bought at an airport convenience store about six years ago. The cards are well broken in but still very crisp and bouncy. We use an old set of poker chips I found in my grandmother's attic as the stake. It's fun. Sometimes I get dealt a great hand, sometimes a lousy one. It doesn't really matter; the chips all even out in the end and I know there are still plenty more poker games to come.

Life is all about playing cards. Estelle Murphy always asks me to play one more game of gin rummy before I leave, for fear that it could be her deck's last. I always do. Jimmy Siegel will have a tough time learning how to play a lot of card games during his lifetime because of the hand he was dealt. But his deck is still brand-new and he can make of it what he wants. It'll just take a little more work. As for my deck, it's still a mystery to me. I'm not sure how my hand will play out, but I'm thankful for all that I've been dealt and I'm taking it day by day. We'll see how the cards fall.

This essay is very accomplished. Anyone would encourage Jeff to use this piece on almost any application. He could have adapted it to almost any prompt. The message is universal. He worked in one of his volunteer activities (the nursing home), some summer work (camp), and his compassion for the aged and disadvantaged into his essay. It's also relatively short. You don't have to drone on and on to make your point known. Conciseness is a virtue.

Inside Tip

Don't underestimate the power of short, declarative sentences. Every one of Jeff's five topic sentences is a simple declarative sentence. One of the common mistakes students make when writing an essay is to use too many long, introductory phrases in their leads. Look at Jeff's third paragraph. It begins: "Jimmy Siegel didn't understand blackjack." Those few words say a lot. They also provide some tension and interest to fuel our continuing involvement with the writing. Some less-practiced writers might have said, "Because of his learning disability, which he had from birth, Jimmy Siegel didn't understand blackjack." What's wrong with that? Be economical in your writing.

Another Cornell statement by Jeff Fine:

Write about your intended field of study.

When I was a year-and-a-half old, I learned to walk. Eventually I became pretty good at it, but at the time I didn't understand why I was walking. What was the theoretical reasoning behind what I was doing? I hadn't a clue. It wasn't until later, after my mind developed further, that I learned it was necessary to walk in order to get from Point A to Point B.

The same could be said for me now, over fifteen years later. As I said before in another essay, I'm a journalist. But *why* am I a journalist? What's the point of journalism? What is communications all about? That's what I aim to find out.

I'm in love with the practical application of the field. No question about it. I'm a journalistic "walker" you might say, even though I know how to "run" a high school newspaper. I've been doing that for more than two years. I think I've done a good job. The state award this year speaks for itself. In any case, I'm still far from understanding the theory behind what makes these things tick.

I can get on the radio once a week, host a show, spin some tunes, and deliver the news. No big deal. I can entertain an audience of my peers with ease. It's the logistics I want to learn. The way I see it, even if I can walk with confidence, intensive experience and instruction will be necessary for me to succeed, to move to the next level. That's why the School of Agriculture and Life Sciences at Cornell is my clear first choice among all the programs I've seen. There's no question that the program is the best fit for me.

One thing I've noticed about my work with our high school paper is that the more challenging the work gets, the more I enjoy it. Cornell could be the most fun yet.

Admissions committees love to read how people face and overcome challenges in their lives. Monica Candal is an overcomer. She wrestled with shyness in her young years.

Monica applied to Brown, Georgetown, Harvard, and Tulane. She was accepted to Brown, Georgetown and Tulane all EA, and Harvard deferred her to regular decision, ultimately denying her admission. Here is Monica's essay.

When I was a young, awkward adolescent, I considered myself to be a shy person, especially around boys. Because of this, my experiences at a coed middle school intimidated me somewhat. So, for the past five years, I have attended an all-girls school, which has helped me to become a stronger person. I have overcome my shyness and insecurities and have developed much more confidence.

Ironically, I believe that my shyness, something that I consider a communication barrier, has ultimately led me to focus on a field for my life's work: communications. Despite my aversion to it early on in life, I now love speaking to and interacting with people, be it as a friend, teacher, or public speaker. I now have a passion for stimulating conversation, and that enthusiasm manifests itself in three different and important aspects of my life outside of the classroom: peer support, volunteer work, and music.

Peer support is a high school-sponsored program through which juniors and seniors are selected to work with eighth graders who attend Sacred Heart. It involves an intensive three-day workshop where student leaders learn how to listen effectively to and become mentors for the younger students. I love this work. Once a week, I get to speak to these impressionable boys and girls about anything that I feel is important. I enjoy learning about their lives and their issues and exploring possible solutions to their problems. We study today's society and its impact on them. I see much of my old self in these young people and that memory has helped me to help them become more confident about their everyday lives.

My volunteer work centers on teaching through a program called Summerbridge. After school, I go to a nearby public school and tutor learning-disadvantaged preteens. Instead of dealing with the students' personal issues, as I do in peer support, the Summerbridge focus is more on communication through education. By working with these younger students, I have come to understand the importance of helping them comprehend and apply what they learn in the classroom. Their motivation, given their circumstances, is remarkable. We discuss in detail what they are learning so that I can keep them interested and motivated. Summerbridge is another example of how communication issues are very important to me.

Not surprisingly, music has emerged as another, perhaps indirect, avenue for me to communicate with others. Singing allows me to convey my deep and personal emotions with others. When I sing, I am transported to another realm. The mundane everyday world around me disappears, and I am enveloped in my own, new space, especially when I am performing onstage. When I act, I am transformed, feeling the happiness, sadness, impishness, or even confusion that my character feels. My performance taps into that part of me where those qualities dwell, and I love sharing it with my audience. Music is a very special form of communication for me.

Perhaps the person I am today is a compensation for who I was years ago. That awkward twelve-year-old, however, is no more. Now I want to show the world what I can do. Communication has become my passion. It will be my future.

Inside Tip

Monica has three things immediately in her favor: culture, compassion, and discipline. Her five years in a private, all-girls school probably demanded a refinement of her social skills. Her tutoring and mentorship experiences are sustained over several years, not simply offered as a bullet-point, one-time-only exposure shared for the sake of filling up an application. She cares and has stick-to-it-ness. Those are qualities that make for successful students and alumni.

Chapter 9

The Waiting Game

You've mailed the application. What do you do now?

You've heard the clichés: "knock on wood" and "cross your fingers." If you're serious about getting into a highly selective college, though, this isn't the time to go back to your life and just wait. Instead, there are a number of strategies you should put into motion to increase your chances of being accepted by being noticed. Let's define that better: you don't want to be an incessant pest, calling the admissions office every other day, or sending a barrage of annoying e-mails to the staff and worse yet (but true—someone has tried this), sending a note to the college president letting him or her know your application is on the way. We're talking about drawing attention to your candidacy among the staff and faculty who have influence during the admission process.

Two Kinds of Applications

In general, there are two kinds of applicants that get accepted to elite schools.

1. Those who do everything right in preparing their applications, send them in on time, and most likely don't need to do anything else in order to be acceptable to the admissions staff. Of course, if you're one of these, you can't know, so you are ecstatic when you receive an acceptance letter.

2. Those who do everything right in preparing their applications, send them in on time, but need to show something extra to the admissions staff in order to be accepted. You don't know this either. You may not ever receive an acceptance letter unless you bring your candidacy up to an equal standing with the first group.

Whether you're actually in the first group or the second, assume that you're in the second. Until you know for sure that you're in or out, you should be consistently proactive while the admissions committee is considering your application.

The Faculty Visit

In some colleges, the admissions decision is either (a) made within the individual department or division to which a student applies; (b) made after the admissions office assembles the initial criteria and pre-qualifies only those the department asked to see by basic academic standards (GPA, SAT, certain coursework taken in high school, etc.); or (c) some combination of these two models. You obviously don't want to be sifted out before faculty ever has a chance to see your credentials.

Make an appointment with a full-time faculty member. You might not get the department chair, but if you get a sympathetic ear, don't play a pathetic role. You aren't there to ask them to look at you closely just because you've applied. You're there to develop an on-campus advocate. How do you do that? You could ask him about internship opportunities to complement your studies if you're accepted, or have him glance at your final draft of a paper or other project for your senior-year class project. Whatever you share, make sure you tie all of your interests directly into the interests of the faculty members and the classes offered at the school. You can find out both of these things on a college's website by browsing course catalogues and the faculty home pages. The point here is to come across as a student who takes her studies seriously. If you're convincing, when the folders come over for review, and yours is not there along with the rest, the professor might actually pick up the phone and say, "I noticed Sue's application isn't here. What's that? She didn't make the first cut? Well, I'd like to see it anyway.

She has some pretty interesting student research going on that might not have been reflected in the application."

The In-Depth Facilities Tour

No generalized tour has the time to take you through the high-tech labs, the backstage area of the performing arts center, the environmental field station and associated labs, or the visual arts facilities in depth. You need to come back and do this yourself. Arrange this directly through a specific department. Tell the department that you are an active applicant and that you would like to see the facilities at a time convenient to the faculty and students. Tell the department that you are considering other top-tier colleges and would like to know specifically why this college's faculty, staff, students, and physical resources are better-suited to undergraduate learning and research. Faculty are almost always delighted when you ask this, because they can sell the specifics of their department better than most admissions staff can. It also shows that you take your studies seriously, so much so that you're checking out what sort of resources will be available to you in the future.

Inside Tip

Send a note to the admissions officer assigned to recruit in your geographic territory or high school. Let him know that you visited campus again and were invited to tour the facilities at whatever department it was. Tell him *after* you've visited, and he will be impressed that you took the time to alert him. Plus, it saves him the embarrassment of not knowing that one of his recruits was talking to faculty.

Alumni Networking

There are some acceptable ways to work with alumni and other partners in your—and the college's—best interests. Here are a couple of examples.

Did you have a terrific internship at a company this past summer and run into an alumna from the college to which you applied? If you did a great job, ask her to write a letter of recommendation for you. Make sure she mentions that you have already applied.

Many admissions offices host information sessions sponsored by alumni chapters across the country. Most often, alumni will hold an informal meet-and-greet session for prospective students and parents. If you are invited to one of these, no matter where it is, go. If you have not yet been invited to any such event, go to the college website and look for regional alumni chapters. If you find contact information, call the local alumni chapter officer and ask if there are events in your region. Get invited. It is rare when a proud alumnus will say "Sorry—we only invite those prospective students the admissions office tells us to." When you show up, act professional and polite, listen well, and learn everything you can from the alumni who speak. You can count on an admissions representative being there, or at least an alumni admissions volunteer. They will take note of your presence and attendance, and most likely pass their notes on to the office. If you were recruited this way, stay in touch this way. Get business cards, e-mails, and other contact information. Send a barrage of personalized thank-you notes, and make sure you keep in touch. Ask alumni you met to look into the status of your application—politely, and only once. While alumni contact isn't always a shoo-in strategy, having a bunch of graduates pulling for you can make a difference.

Selling yourself isn't guaranteed to work. If you get the signal from one or more of your contacts that your self-marketing is no longer necessary, thank everyone you can remember who gave you an ear or advice. If you're denied admission or waitlisted, you never know when a call might come and your candidacy will be looked at again.

Remember, if you followed everything in the application instructions, the admissions office has everything they need on paper. It's your job to personalize yourself beyond the paperwork.

Chapter *10*

Rejection, Deferrals, and Waitlists: Plan B

Rejection ≠ Dejection

Getting a rejection letter from a college or university doesn't make you a bad person. Most high schoolers tend to take being turned down by a college or university on a personal level. They seem to think that the letter from the admissions office is really saying something like, "You aren't worth it, and we don't want to have anything to do with you." Nothing could be farther from the truth.

Such is the case with many good colleges. Everyone who is good enough to get in isn't always offered admission. Take a little time to feel disappointed about not getting into your most-desired school. Don't dwell on it, though. Don't hate those schools forever. Don't view successful candidates at those schools as elitist snobs. Accept the fact that you didn't make the cut—for whatever reason—and get on with your life. Look at the schools that have accepted you. Select the one that best suits your needs and prepare to have a great higher education experience. Yes, there is life after rejection, but how can you head off rejection at the pass?

The High-Price Spread

The oracle at Delphi advises all who visit to "know thyself." That's exceptional advice for college applicants. Your college-application strategy should begin with an honest appraisal of how you stack up as a competitive applicant. A frank assessment early on can save you much rejection grief down the road. How can you do this?

The first step is to develop a reasonable list of college candidates. It's surprising how many seniors overlook the obvious advantages of spreading the risk by deciding on a list that is ridiculously top heavy. A top-heavy list might include the usual suspects: Harvard, Yale, Princeton, Stanford, MIT, Williams, Amherst, Swarthmore, and so on. Sometimes students will throw in a hastily picked safety just in case.

A spread like this is way out of balance. Our advice to you is to do a serious, unbiased evaluation of your academic, extracurricular, and writing skills. Consider where you live (students from Butte, Montana have a better chance of getting into Brown than those from Cambridge, Massachusetts), whether your school is public or private, and your current grade. Closely study your academic credentials: current GPA (weighted and unweighted), class rank, test scores (SATs [I and II] and ACT), and your current course schedule. How many Advanced Placement courses have you taken and what did you score on the exams?

As for extracurriculars, you need to examine the nature of your activities and the length and depth of your involvement. You should do the same with your volunteer work. Honors are important, as are summer activities and jobs.

Finally, you need to consider any legacy connections you may have with any of your candidate schools.

Take all of the answers to these questions and plug them into Counselor-o-Matic on www.review.com. Counselor-o-Matic will return a list of fifteen schools (five reaches, five ballpark or target schools, and five safety schools) to which you should apply. Of course, Counselor-o-Matic doesn't guarantee that you will get into any school it suggests, since it can't evaluate less quantifiable things.

Sometimes students who appear to be not all that outstanding from a numbers standpoint can be amazing writers. You've already seen the value of essay efforts, as well as tips on how to put forth a great one yourself, in Chapter 8.

Keep Your Balance

If your overall profile is close to that of the admitted first-year students at your candidate colleges (information available on www.review.com), you'll know that you at least have a chance. As mentioned before, though, don't just go by numbers alone. There are also the essays, your recommendations, your application packaging, and intangibles.

A minimum of five to six colleges on a candidate list (two reaches, maybe three or four targets, and a safety or two) is a practical plan. Your list should *not* include HYPSM plus your local state university. That's just irresponsible and foolish.

Plan B

Let's say that your Plan A consists of an ED application to your first-choice school. For Graham from Chapter 7, it was Stanford. Most ED programs have a deadline that falls somewhere around November 1 to November 15. Since your ED application represents your best effort, you'll already have great material to complete your Plan B applications if they become necessary.

There is anywhere from a four- to six-week waiting period for finding out about early applications. They go in to colleges by early November, and colleges send out their letters by mid-December. What can you do to help your admission process during this empty time? Sit back and hope for the best? Yeah, right.

Let's assume that your list of colleges looks something like this:

First-choice early-decision school: Swarthmore College

Other reaches: Williams, Trinity, and Haverford

Ballpark candidates: Bard, Bucknell, and Lafayette

Safeties: Denison University and home-state university's main campus

Here's what you'll need to do to make the most of this in-between time.

Get all of your candidate schools' applications as soon as possible. You conserve a lot of energy and ideas if you have all of your applications in front of you at one time, early in the application season. Since Swarthmore is your early-apply school, look at the essay(s) you'll be required to write. Chances are, the main essay prompt will be something along the lines of "Tell us something about yourself that we can't learn from the other parts of your application."

There may also be some shorter questions asking for specific information such as "What is it about Swarthmore that motivated you to apply?" These types of specific-information questions usually require original answers and don't lend themselves to recycling. Be careful. If you try to adapt college-specific statements to other applications, you could end up committing application suicide. Don't cut and paste your way into the reject pile.

You might be able to get away with writing just one major essay that can satisfy the main-essay prompts of all your applications. This is much more likely if your early-application school has a general essay prompt of the "tell us something" variety. You can also get a lot of other details out of the way all at once, like your personal and statistical data.

Brief your recommenders about your application strategy. Since you won't be finding out about your early application until mid-December, that leaves only a couple of weeks until most of your other applications' RD deadlines (usually the first of January). Notice anything else about those two weeks? Yep, they're sitting there like toads, right in the middle of your winter break. It's going to be your teachers' winter break too. They're not going to appreciate having to generate more recommendations for you if you come running to them after a deferral letter arrives on December 15.

That's why you should tell everyone—your teachers, your counselor, your summer-job supervisor, or whomever—what to expect, especially about your Plan B. Chances are, most of them will have their letters on a computer file. They can just change the date and the school's name and address and print out a new copy.

Have your RD applications on deck and ready to go by mid-December. Do you really want to spend your winter break scrambling to complete the remainder of your Plan B applications?

If you want to relax on your *vacation*, have those other apps ready to roll before you get the not-so-good news from your early-apply school(s). Obviously, if you're accepted early decision, or get into one or more of your multiple early-action schools, that's all the good news you need. On the other hand, if you get the dreaded deferral or, worse yet, get rejected, you're going to be disappointed but at least you won't have to generate new and enthusiastic applications while moping. Your already completed Plan B will have taken care of all that.

Deferrals and Waitlists

If you're waitlisted, you'll have to make a decision: Do you want to stay on the waitlist or pursue other options and enroll elsewhere? In most cases, there's no concrete termination point for your waitlist uncertainty. It could drag on into the summer after you graduate. If the self-marketing plan we're about to describe doesn't have any positive effect on your status, we can almost guarantee you that, barring a miracle, you're not going to be admitted. If that's the case, withdraw your application and apply elsewhere.

So, what's this great self-marketing plan? It's all about finding a key contact at the school that has deferred or waitlisted you and feeding that person carefully planned information about your accomplishments and passion for that school. Here is your plan, step-by-step:

1. Find out the name of the person who has authority over your application. In most cases, this will be the regional admissions representative for your area of the country. Start searching for this person immediately. Do not put this off. You can find out who she is in several ways. First, you can check the school's website. Most colleges have a separate page or segment of their site devoted to undergraduate admissions. In some cases, depending on the size of the school, they may have the admission officers' names, their geographic assignment, and (if you're really lucky) their e-mail address.

If this information isn't available on the school's website, then you'll have to call the admissions office. Don't chicken out here. You've got to remember that you get one shot at the process, and this is it. Don't let mom or dad do the talking. If an admissions officer ends up speaking with one of your parents, she'll immediately think that you don't have the commitment or maturity to handle this important task for yourself.

2. State your case. Make your first contact with your rep by telephone. Be organized and to the point. Tell your rep that you're calling to get some perspective on your deferral or waitlisting. In most cases, the rep will retrieve your folder or look up your data on their computer while you're on the line. She'll do a quick review of her notes and be as forthcoming as possible about why you were deferred or waitlisted. Some reps even comment on the degree of deferral. That is, she might say something like, "You were a high deferral," or

something similar. If you hear a positive comment like this, get charged up.

Tell your rep that you're still extremely interested in attending that college and that you'd like to stay in touch. Regardless of how you put this, as long as you sound sincere, your rep will understand what you mean. She'll make note of it. And remember that little pluses add up.

3. Schedule your contacts and updates. If you've been deferred, you're going to have about three months before the college sends you a final decision. You'll want to make about three to six contacts with your rep in this time period, depending on how much update news you can generate. You don't want your rep to feel that you're a pest. If you have something to say, then say it, but don't just talk to hear yourself talk. A brief e-mail or call every two or three weeks ought to do it.

4. Turn up the academic heat. This is mainly for those who have been deferred from an early application. Remember that you submitted your application in early November and learned of your deferral in mid-December. There's an early-February midyear report waiting to go in on you that shows your academic progress for the first half of the school year. Obviously, if possible, you want to show some positive improvement.

You should also consider entering or completing any competitions that involve your specialties, be they writing, poetry, speech, moot court, or whatever. Your goal is to position yourself as a strong finisher, someone who has not yet realized his or her full potential.

5. Scout for an additional recommendation. Whoever this is must know you at least as well as those who wrote your initial recs. For example, if it's your employer, ask him or her to mention specifics about your work or performance. As with your other recommendations, anecdotal information is crucial. A well-done extra recommendation like this can sometimes prove to be crucial.

Bottom line: Don't put your brain to bed. Use it. All this new information can be worked into your regular updates with your admissions contact. The overall impression you're trying to project is that you're a young man or woman sitting on the fence showing one heck of a lot of spirit and intelligence about getting into this school. Because the majority of deferred and waitlisted applicants are content to just sit and wait, you'll stand out from the crowd.

Northwestern University Photographer

Northwestern University, located near Chicago in Evanston, Illinois, is an exceedingly selective school of just under 8,000 undergraduates. One of Northwestern's most popular majors is journalism, no doubt due to its famous Medill School of Journalism. NU sports compete in the Big Ten conference against the likes of Penn State, Ohio State, Michigan, and other national powerhouses. There's lots of school spirit and student social life is strongly influenced by NU's dominant fraternity and sorority scene.

Chapter 11

The Money Monster

If you've been accepted to one or more of your top-choice colleges or universities, CONGRATULATIONS!

But wait. Can you afford the college of your dreams? Most applicants and their parents wait with as much trepidation for financial aid award letters as they do for a notification of acceptance. And those financial award letters carry almost as much weight as the acceptance letters themselves. Ultimately, the net cost of attendance is the biggest influence on a student's final decision on where to go to college.

If we hit the mark, you should walk away from this chapter knowing (1) how to discover what criteria your elite college of choice uses to determine the amount of scholarship (read: free) money it awards you, (2) what you should think about before negotiating a financial aid offer, and (3) how to approximate what four years of schooling will ultimately cost you and your family.

How Colleges Determine What to Give You

Here's a basic template for you to use. As we discuss each issue, you may want to start building a profile for how the financial aid office of each of the schools you're planning on applying to might treat your information by jotting a note down next to each criterion.

	<u>College A</u>	<u>College B</u>	<u>College C</u>
Financial Aid: What does the college use to determine financial awards? How?			
EFC (Expected Family Contribution)			
Application Deadline Status (Early, Regular)			
GPA			
SAT/ACT			
AP Classes/Honors/College Prep			
Service and Volunteer Activities			
Cocurricular Activities			
Interview			
Essays			
Recommendations			
Alumni Status			
Special Considerations and Preferences			

When to Apply and Why
Early Decision and Binding Agreements
Can colleges tell if you've pulled your application? Yes, they have a variety of means of discovering if you have. And if the college provides a financial aid award with your acceptance, how do you know if the offer you'd have received from other colleges would have been better? You obviously can't know the answer to these questions, and that's the risk you take when applying ED.

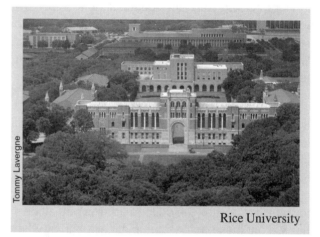

Rice University

Grade Point Average
No matter what you read about the SAT or ACT, almost all colleges look at your GPA as the number-one measure of academic performance. Just how do colleges use GPA to determine a scholarship? There are three major ways colleges evaluate your GPA.

- Take the GPA the school registrar supplies on your official high school transcript. On a four-point scale, for example, a 3.75 is a 3.75, with no regard for the courses you took. It makes no difference that you got all As in gym class, wood shop, theatre and religion classes, and a B in each of your geometry, chemistry, and history classes.

- Take the academic courses and average them independently of all other courses. In this case, a college will look for college preparatory classes in English, mathematics, social science, life sciences, and foreign languages. If your overall GPA is 3.75, but you received lower grades in the academic courses than you did in all other courses, admission officers might recalculate your GPA and use that number as the measure of both college readiness and for deciding your merit-based scholarship. How do you know what they use? Ask them at the beginning of your college search. It might change your mind about what you decide to take in your next semester.

- Take AP and honors-level courses and weight them higher than the stated grade. You need to know if your high school submits your grades to colleges as reported on your report card or weights them to include the AP and honors-level courses at a higher value. If they do not weight AP and honors-level courses higher, ask the college admissions office if they weight these grades automatically, and by what factor. You obviously want an admissions committee to use your highest possible GPA. Here are two examples of how this might look inside the admission office.

College A does not weight AP courses				College B weights AP courses x 1.25			
Course	Grade	Units	Points	Course	Grade	Units	Points
Chemistry	B	39.0	9.0	Chemistry	B	3.0	9.0
AP English	A	4.0	16.0	AP English	A	4.0	17.0
AP Biology	B	3.0	9.0	AP Biology	B	3.0	9.75
US History	A	4.0	16.0	US History	A	4.0	16.0
Band	A	1.0	4.0	Band	A	1.0	4.0
Average (points/units):			3.6	Average (points/units):			3.72

Inside Tip

Unless you are determined to apply early decision, do not file your application until you know you have achieved the highest possible GPA you can present on your transcripts. Most colleges that accept a student on the basis of a completed application use the transcripts submitted at the time of application. If you should achieve a higher overall GPA in the marking periods following your acceptance, few colleges will adjust your merit-based scholarship to reflect the higher GPA. This is especially true of the early decision applicant who is accepted, receives a financial aid package, accepts it, and pays a matriculation deposit.

Other Factors Influencing Merit Awards

SAT/ACT

While a few schools use the SAT or ACT alone to determine merit-based scholarships, most start with a basic matrix, where the student's test score is set on one axis, and his or her GPA is on the other. Here's a simplified example of one model that correlates SAT scores with various GPAs to determine a merit-based scholarship:

	GPA			
SAT	3.75–4.00	3.50–3.74	3.25–3.49	< 3.25
1400–1600	$15,000	$12,500	$10,000	$7,500
1350–1390	$12,500	$10,000	$7,500	$5,000
1280–1320	$10,000	$7,500	$5,000	$4,000
1200–1270	$7,500	$5,000	$4,000	$2,500

Much like for-profit companies, even elite colleges usually rely on statistical models to determine what specific scholarship levels will result in the largest number of students who send in a deposit. Just because an elite college draws an enormous number of qualified applicants doesn't mean that the best students will end up in their freshman class. In fact, America's most prestigious colleges boast a very low acceptance rate, while their yield on accepted students (number who are accepted that actually deposit and matriculate) is generally between 20–40% of the total accepted.[1] A college's list price minus all scholarships, grants, and other self-help sources is the single greatest determinant of yield. Colleges know this. And since the most highly qualified students will be accepted to the most schools, colleges offer them more money as an enticement to enroll. It's symbiotic: The student has to pay less to attend, and the college gets a boost to its freshman academic profile.

[1] A select few of America's elite colleges have yield rates significantly higher than 40%.

Bottom line: Ask a financial aid office which scholarships are automatically awarded to all students accepted within a certain GPA range and standardized test score range.

Volunteer Activities

It's rare that a college offers scholarships on the basis of the number of volunteer activities a student lists in his or her application. Instead, it tries to look for the ways in which your service leadership potential might be accommodated within its academic and community program offerings. The relationship between the admissions office and the fundraising and alumni relations offices is close. The former is often called upon to recruit specific students for any number of scholarships endowed by wealthy alumni.

Inside Tip

Try to locate alumni or current students who have a connection with the development (fundraising) office at your elite college of choice. Many scholarships have criteria that focus on students who, in addition to presenting admirable academic criteria, have been actively engaged in volunteer service work. Some of these scholarships also link service work with specific academic majors. Others are earmarked for needy students. Find out about as many scholarships as you can and match them up with your own academic, financial, and service background.

Cocurriculars

Much like service-oriented scholarships, awards made available to top athletic recruits are plentiful, and available to both needy and well-off students. The National Collegiate Athletic Association (www.ncaa.org) is specific about the scholarship parameters at Division I and II schools. Division III schools do not offer athletic scholarships.

Some colleges offer a myriad of talent-based scholarships in musical and theatrical performance, the fine arts, and other academically related areas. Some also offer scholarships in designated disciplines such as environmental science, premedicine, public policy and prelaw, economics and business, and education. Each of these relies not only on a student's basic academic performance, but also take into consideration the student's involvement in related activities in high school and out-of-class experiences.

Bottom Line: The awarding of scholarships and other forms of financial aid, like the decision to accept a student in the first place, is not about what a college owes you. It's an issue about what you, the student, can offer a college community. In other words, if you are a fantastic violin player, but the college orchestra already has four first-chair–caliber violin players, trying to win a scholarship by emphasizing your violin talent probably won't yield positive results.

Inside Tip

Many endowed scholarships are administered by the financial aid office in consultation with the donor who provided the principal funding for the scholarship. If you can find out more about the donor's wishes, you might be able to shape your activities to more closely match what the donor wants to see. Be careful. Contact with a donor could cause the college to disqualify you from consideration for a scholarship. You might be able to find out more from an upperclassman who has already benefited from the scholarship you're after. In any case, be honest about your volunteer and service activities, and in the case of major-specific scholarships, find out how, what, why, when, and where current students became eligible for the specific scholarship source that seems to be a match for your passion.

Financial Planning 101

Colleges construct a financial aid award using three components: (1) merit scholarships, (2) need-based grants, and (3) self-help. You want to know what they use so you can figure out how to afford the four years of attendance. Colleges must have enough full-paying students to enroll along with students who demonstrate great financial need because most schools don't have endowments large enough (or full support from the government) to allow them to give everyone a free ride. They count on tuition revenue, along with other sources of income, just to run their administrative and educational operations.

This is a complex issue, and there is no way we could completely explain it to you in this book. What we can do, though, is give you an idea of how colleges manage their financial issues internally.

Merit scholarships are intended to reward a student for academic achievement in high school and extracurricular involvement. Colleges have different definitions of "achievement" and various methods of awarding merit scholarships. Some colleges don't offer merit awards to families without financial need. Others limit merit scholarships to nonathletes. Check with the colleges you're considering for the exact method they use to determine your eligibility, if any, for the various merit scholarships they offer.

Grants, on the other hand, are need-based. Like merit scholarships, grants do not have to be paid back to a college. Grants are more subject to change over each of your four years of college than merit scholarships, as you and your family's finances can change dramatically from one year to the next. Merit scholarships usually remain the same for each year no matter how you and your family's finances change.

Self-help includes all other financial sources, such as loans and work-study. When all forms of aid are compiled for a particular student, the remaining net cost of enrollment is the expected family contribution (EFC). The total self-help award, even though it may include loans on which the parent or student must begin repayment while the student is still matriculated, is not lumped into the EFC.

EFC, Scholarships, Grants, Self-Help, and the Bottom Line

Your goal is to reduce the net cost of attendance for each of the colleges you're considering. Once you know the system each college uses to determine your EFC, the decision about which college to attend is primarily one of value. Weigh the net cost of each college against what you and your family consider to be the most important things each school can contribute to your education. The college that matches your values, needs, and goals and offers the most reasonable net cost for those values will most likely be the one you choose to attend.

List Price vs. Net Cost

During the 1990s, the cost of tuition increased dramatically, even doubling at some schools. So has the cost of housing, automobiles, condos and vacation homes, and quite a few other durable, tangible goods and services. This is a good point for an illustrative story.

The Case of the SUV, Boat, and Trailer People

Several years ago David, as an enrollment officer, spent an hour in his office with a father and his son. The young man had been accepted to the college David was serving at the time, and he and Dad were there to negotiate a better offer of financial aid. This tag-team of father and son, for whatever reason, had been conditioned to believe that "your college wants my son, so if you want him (his money), you'll have to do better than the college down the road." After all, the father said, colleges owed his son something for all he accomplished in high school and in his community over the past three years. He wanted David to match three other college financial aid offers that were all seemingly $1,000 cheaper per year, yet the college David represented was his son's first choice.

David looked out the window at the family car. It was a fairly new Ford Explorer, *Eddie Bauer* edition, complete with a very nice inboard engine pleasure boat and custom trailer, headed for the local lake after this campus visit. David asked, "Is that your SUV and boat out there?"

"Yep. Just bought it. Isn't it a beauty?"

"Well, yes," said David, "but help me here. How much is the entire rig worth, boat and all, if you don't mind me asking?"

"The whole thing was about $50,000. We got a great deal, though."

"Did you pay cash?" David asked.

"No, we floated a five-year note at 8%, with only a few hundred down!"

"Let me understand this. You're willing to pay $50,000 for a pleasure vehicle and boat, financed over just five years, for something that loses value immediately, and has little residual value after the loan is paid off, including interest charges. And you don't plan on keeping it long after that, do you?"

"Well, no. By that time, I'm guessing the newest models will be out. Why do you ask?"

"I think that our conversation is more about what you consider an investment for short-term pleasure versus an investment that pays a lifetime of rewards. Yet you say that you are unwilling to pay just $1,000 more for an education we know is worth more than an SUV and a boat."

His son wanted to crawl under a rock. Dad looked down, then smiled and said something that sounded like, "Yeah, you're right." Dad paid the deposit, and his son graduated on time. David saved $1,000 that didn't need to be invested in a family that didn't have the need for the extra scholarship dollars.

The Moral of the Story

There is an upper limit to what colleges will provide students within various need and quality parameters. The ceiling is the total amount of aid, from all sources, that can be awarded to a student. What factors establish the ceiling? Financial need, as determined by the U.S Department of Education (FAFSA) is one component. Another is academic quality, determined by the individual college on its own unique criteria. Special considerations, such as alumni relationships, athletic ability, musical or art talent, and minority status can be found in the models colleges use to determine who gets what financial aid. Finally, various complex computations that predict the yield on all accepted students (both those who are offered need-based aid and those who don't need or don't qualify for aid) are part of the business of predicting and ensuring a tuition-revenue–producing freshman class year after year.

Let's look at a few models to help you compare financial aid offers. We'll finish up with a few tips on how to understand the long-term implications of your financial investment and talk about a little-known feature many colleges have employed to manage enrollment, the four-year guarantee.

Understanding Your Financial Award

Once you have received your award, it's time to look at the real cost of your education. That is, don't just look at the first year's costs. Think about future costs, increases in tuition, and the costs associated with interest rates on loans you accept as part of your package, as well as the hidden costs of managing your investments and savings. The following examples are hypothetical, but based upon real experiences and actual packaging issues. Illustrations for each example can be found on pages 170–172.

Example 1

In this example, although the colleges have similar list prices, it appears that the family's direct costs (those that require cash, check, or other immediate payment source each semester) are slightly different. College A seems to be cheaper if you are looking at the amount of direct costs to the student/family at the top of the column, or the EFC. The merit awards (scholarships primarily based upon academic achievement) are different, as are the amount of grant aid and loans offered to the family as part of the total aid package. In the first column, the college has offered a larger merit-based award, but a smaller grant to this family with financial need. The loan is also larger, which means that, depending on the interest rate of the loan and whether or not it's subsidized, College A could end up costing more than College B. Work-study rounds out the package.

Example 2

In this example, the first column shows a larger merit award, a smaller need-based grant, and a nominal amount of loan. The second column depicts a much smaller merit award, a larger need-based grant, and a loan amount equal to the first column. Work-study again rounds out each package.

Analyzing Offers of Aid

Look again at Example 1. If you think immediate (direct) costs are less each year for college A, specifically because the merit-based grant offered is larger, then look again. Two issues exist that could change your thinking.

First, depending upon the loan source, the true cost of the loan is both the principal and the interest paid over the life of the loan period. Some families find it wiser to pay the interest, or pay off a college loan early, than pull other assets out or an investment option that is earning great returns. Don't forget the loss of interest earned by using other investments to pay down college loans.

Second, the financial aid offered in the beginning of a student's freshman year can change for one or more of the following academic years. And in many of these cases, it is not because the family's financial circumstances changed. It's not uncommon to see the need-based grant of a student's financial award reduced and a loan or other self-help source offered in its place. Yes, there are always restrictions, and to be fair to colleges nationwide, students often bear responsibility for the loss of scholarship, grant, or other fund source, most often by not keeping up academically with the required standards. In some cases, though, a college might experience a change in fiscal policy and must in turn change the combination of funds awarded in the continuing student's financial package. Look again at Example 2. It is possible that in succeeding years, the need-based grant amount listed for "Private College B" could change to self-help loans or simply be added to the family's direct costs. This would make "Private College B" cost more over the four-year period than originally depicted in Example 2. Ethically, a college should communicate this to you well in advance and give solid reasons why the college must take this course of action.

Take a look at Example 3. Unlike the first two examples, which depict offers of aid at two different schools, Example 3 shows a financial aid package at the same college for the first two years. In this case, the family took on the responsibility of the loss of half the need-based grant in the sophomore year. This difference might show up as an award of another loan, too, not just direct costs.

If a college guarantees the same aid package for all four years (see explanation below), you should challenge any changes, especially in a reduction of need-based grants in your award. There should be no surprises. Likewise, you should be up-front and with the financial aid office when your finances change for better or worse. The college financial aid office will pick up on your financial status one way or another, and it's easier for everyone to work out the details early on rather than surprising the other with new dramatic changes to the previous semester's bill late in the game.

Inside Tip

Many merit-based scholarships require specific measures of academic progress or other enrollment status. For example, to maintain a top scholarship to study physics, you might be required to maintain a 3.75 or better each academic year, in either the major, the core courses in physics, or overall GPA. Additionally, if you change your major, few colleges would continue to subsidize you with a physics scholarship to study fine arts.

Bottom line: ask the financial aid office what academic progress restrictions there are on the merit-based scholarship you're seeking. If it's a hard-and-fast GPA requirement, ask if students are notified well in advance that they are close to losing a portion or all of the scholarship when their grades slip. Also ask if it is standard practice to require a student to develop a plan of study to show they are working on improving their grades. This is a growing trend among colleges who understand that the threat of pulling financial aid is not a very effective method of encouraging good scholarship, and can only lead to stress for students and their families.

The Four-Year Guarantee

Here's another trend that helps students and families plan for the total cost of education over the long haul: the four-year guarantee. With this guarantee, unless your financial circumstances change, you will receive aid right through graduation. This is a particularly fair and progressive way of approaching student financial planning, but it does have its loopholes and drawbacks.

- **Conditions and Terms.** This phrase usually is found on a form each college sends out to students with their award packages. For scholarships, it spells out the conditions that must be met academically and financially. If your financial need changes, your eligibility for grants might change as well. Let's say that you hit the state lottery for $40 million. You can expect your need to disappear somewhere down the line, perhaps as soon as your very next semester bill. You must document and communicate every change in your financial status to the college's aid office.

- **Increases in Tuition, Room, Board and Required Fees.** Do you know what the college of your choice plans to do with your financial aid if tuition increases (and it almost always does)? Just ask current students or their parents. For no-need students, it's usually a matter of paying the difference as it's added each semester to the bill. For students with need met by need-based grants and perhaps by scholarships, a number of things might occur. The college might

a) match the total tuition increase with an equal percentage of grant assistance

b) assume a portion of the increase, and expect you to assume the rest

c) expect you to assume the entire increase each year

Bottom line: Find out what the deal is before you accept your aid award. These are the unexpected costs that can make the difference when choosing between two colleges to which you have been accepted, all other things being equal.

Whew! We hope this makes some sense of the college financial aid process for you. The decision about what you should value is best left up to you.

EXAMPLE 1

Private College A	Private College B
List Price = $30,000	List Price = $30,000

Private College A

Family's Direct Costs
$5,000

Merit-Based Award
$11,000

Need-Based Grant
$4,000

Work-Study
$1,500

Loans
$8,500

Private College B

Family's Direct Costs
$10,000

Merit-Based Award
$8,500

Need-Based Grant
$5,000

Work-Study
$1,500

Loans
$5,000

EXAMPLE 2

Private College A	Private College B
List Price = $30,000	List Price = $30,000

Private College A	Private College B
Family's Direct Costs $5,000	Family's Direct Costs $5,000
Merit-Based Award $15,000	Merit-Based Award $10,000
Need-Based Grant $5,000	Need-Based Grant $10,000
Work-Study $1,500	Work-Study $1,500
Loans $3,500	Loans $3,500

Example 3

Freshman Year	Sophomore Year
List Price = $30,000	List Price = $30,000

Family's Direct Costs $5,000	Family's Direct Costs $10,000
Merit-Based Award $10,000	Merit-Based Award $10,000
Need-Based Grant $10,000	Need-Based Grant $5,000
Work-Study $1,500	Work-Study $1,500
Loans $3,500	Loans $3,500

Chapter 12

Loose Ends and the Days of Summer

Loose Ends

Now is a good time to take care of these. If you've finally finished with your applications, no matter what the outcome has been, take a moment to list everyone who has helped you in the least bit, from those who wrote recommendations for you, to those who helped you craft and rework your essay, to your parents. Now write everyone a thank-you note. Your application required effort from a lot of people who wanted to see you succeed, not just yourself. If you don't take the time to thank people, they might not be around the next time you're looking for a helping hand, like when you're applying to law school or medical school. These notes don't have to be long-winded, just succinct and sincere.

Summer Strategies

Oh, yeah. What about the summer between high school and college? What to do? For most, summertime is probably work time. Most high schoolers start looking for jobs in the early spring, around March. That's when most businesses that want summer help start looking for applicants. Keep in mind that the closer you get to summer, the more desirable jobs become more scarce, having already been picked off by the early birds.

If you're a sophomore, junior, or senior-to-be and you don't have concrete plans for summer work, you can still get a lot done in three months. Summer is an excellent time to prepare for the fall's standardized tests.

You can do this a few ways. First, you can read more quality books. During the summer, many students seem to turn off their brains and settle in for three months of video games. Don't be one of those. Go to the library and check out some classics or poetry. Stimulate your brain. Even if you can make it through only one good book, you're helping yourself. And, like your English teachers always tell you, if you run across words you don't know, look them up in a dictionary.

You could also take some free practice tests on www.princetonreview.com or pick up a copy of *Cracking the SAT* or *Cracking the ACT*. Work through it at your own pace. You've got three months, so there's no need to cram.

Internships

Be creative here. More and more high school students look into summer internships in the fields in which they're interested. You might not make as much money interning as you could waiting tables, but internships *always* look good on the ol' resume, whether you're applying to graduate school or for your first job out of college. Starting early always helps, since each internship can generate one more recommendation letter for you. Besides, showing that you're willing to feed a passion with a low-paying (or no-paying) internship impresses future employers and the admissions committees you've yet to face.

Epilogue

The Hardest Part
Is Getting In

The most challenging part of your college experience will probably be getting into your first choice school. Graduating may be much easier.

The pressure to apply early mounts every admissions season and this year's seniors will face tougher competition than last year's, but not as tough as next year's. No end to the trend is in sight.

In an informative article in the *Yale Daily News* this past year, a student reporter wrote about the increasing number of early applications to elite colleges. Yale's acceptance rate fell from 36 to 29% for early applicants as opposed to last year's overall acceptance rate of 16%. In general, when comparing 16% to 29%, Yale applicants might figure that they have a better than 80% advantage if they apply early. That logic is flawed, but that's how some seniors think, driving up the number of early applications.[1]

The article noted that the number of early applicants to Harvard's early applications increased slightly, lowering the early acceptance rate from 19% to 18%. Compare this to Harvard's frightening 11% overall acceptance rate from last year (a 64% better chance for EA applicants?).

This means that if you're deadly serious about getting into one of America's elite colleges, you're going to have a lot of well-prepared competition. To beat them, you're going to have to be savvy and start early.

You probably read this book for one of two basic reasons. You've either already decided that you're going to apply to an ultra-selective college, or you're thinking about it and wanted to see just how hard it could be. If yours is the second reason, don't be scared away.

[1] Naomi Massave, "Across Ivies, Students Increasingly Apply Early." *Yale Daily News*, January 22, 2001.

Keep in mind that you can never be sure exactly what the admissions office is looking for each year when it bores through those thousands of applications. As you're working on your apps, though, remember that elite colleges in general want smart students with talent and passion.

If you've waited to send in your application until you finished this book, now is the time to go back and check everything one last time. Above all, you should be looking for clarity and consistency. Make sure that your transcripts agree with every recommendation that has gone (or will go) into the admissions office, that your SAT or ACT scores reflect the ability demonstrated by your transcripts, and that your essay is an airtight story of you that makes your candidacy impossible to ignore.

Now make a copy of the whole thing, slap on the correct postage, and drop it in the mail. And enjoy the rest of your senior year.

Appendix I

a) Underrepresented Groups
b) Artists/Musicians
c) Athletes
d) All of the Above

Let's say you've looked at the profiles in the back of this book to compare your own academic and test performance with those of last year's freshmen. If you've found that you don't quite meet the mark, do not close the book. If you're one, some, or all of the above, you've got a much better chance at getting in than you may think.

Excellent at Everything

America's elite colleges have earned their reputations of excellence. They've worked hard to admit the most talented high school seniors, employ the world's most renowned intellectuals, and develop endowments the size of some small countries' GDP. And they are always striving to be more competitive and prestigious in any way they can. They're not content with just being considered academically powerful. They want to be excellent at everything, and that starts with offering the best of everything to their student bodies.

How do underrepresented groups, artists/musicians, and athletes play into a college's plan of being excellent at everything? We repeat over and over how important it is for applicants to understand that these schools admit students who offer something to their campus. If you're one, some, or all of the above, you offer something to a college that most of the kids in their applicant pool don't. And that could be the reason you get admitted over another student with higher test scores and grades than you.

a) Underrepresented Groups

Just what the heck does this mean? If you are from an under-represented group, it means that you are either economically, racially, ethnically, geographically, socially—or any combination of these—different from the majority of the student body. It might sound like a ten-dollar phrase colleges use to refer to minorities these days in light of all the debate over affirmative action. But "underrepresented groups" refers to more than just minorities.

Most applicants to these schools are white kids who grew up in cities and whose parents were moderately well-off financially and went to college themselves. That sounds like a very broad category. It is, and that's the point. If you don't match up to all of these characteristics, though, you're already part of an underrepresented group. If you're a person of color, or grew up in a rural environment, or don't have parents with a college degree, you can offer something unique to a school. Your experience hasn't been that of the white, urban, middle- to upper-class kid, and you'll therefore be able to bring different, refreshing perspectives to the student body and the campus community as a whole. You'll help to contribute to the worldliness of a world-class institution.

Admissions officers know that students who don't meet the characteristics of their typical applicant often aren't exposed to the same academic privileges and encouragement. They now know that the SAT is biased against minorities, and that many kids have parents who can't afford personal tutors or SAT prep courses. If you're from an underrepresented group, your application will get a closer look from an admissions officer, even if you don't have grades and scores as high as most admitted students. They know that you've had to work with the odds stacked against you.

Don't think that you'll have to put forth anything less than your best effort in your application, though. And if you do get admitted to your first-choice school and decide to attend, keep in mind that you could often feel like a fish out of water.

b) Artists/Musicians

We put on music before we started writing this section.Why? Music inspires us. So do good movies. So do good plays. And we're not the only ones; the arts inspire most people. Artists are the world's impact people. Colleges know this, and they want impact people as alumni and students who will inspire their classmates and do great things when they graduate.

Excellence in an art or music is proof in itself of a student's dedication, discipline, and maybe even genius. It isn't hard to understand why the best schools in America would want these types of people attending their classes and living in their residence halls.They, like students from underrepresented groups, contribute to the worldliness of a campus.Admissions officers, as well as the faculty of specific departments, will give an artist's or musician's application a very close look, again, even if he has grades and scores lower than those of most other applicants.

c) Athletes

Over the past several decades, elite colleges have become more and more interested in taking their reputation for academic excellence and extending it to their athletic programs. Did you watch the NCAA men's basketball tournament at all in 2001? A few of the schools profiled in this book advanced pretty far, including Duke, Stanford, and Georgetown. Duke ended up walking away with a national championship.

A college's desire for athletic excellence doesn't just apply to the high-profile men's sports of football and basketball, either. Elite colleges want swimming, track, soccer, lacrosse, golf, baseball, volleyball, and crew teams—men's *and* women's—that kick ass. In terms of the public, athletic success provides a double-edged sword to colleges. First, when college teams are doing well, more alumni attend school social functions, and donations to the school go up. Second, when a high-profile team has an exceptional season or series of seasons, applications to the school increase, obviously making it more selective. In terms of the campus itself, nothing builds school spirit better than a successful athletic team. Recruited athletes, those whom the coaches realize have serious talent, get a lot of leeway in the admissions office. They won't admit just anyone, though. They want to make sure that you can succeed in the classroom too. You, like any other special admissions cases, are going to need to display a respectable high school academic performance. If you're a current high school athlete and you want to learn more about the whole recruiting and admissions process, check out our *Student Athlete's Guide to College.*

Elite College Profiles

America's Elite Colleges

We based our choice of the thirty-two colleges profiled here solely on our selectivity rating. The formula that generates the rating takes into account certain pertinent admissions statistics each school provides us every year. We consider five variables: 1) the percent of students enrolled who come from out-of-state, 2) average standardized test scores of admitted students, 3) the percent of students attending the school from the top ten percent of their high school class, 4) the acceptance rate, and 5) the percentage of students accepted that enrolled. The variables are not necessarily weighted in that order. Those thirty-two four-year colleges with the highest selectivity ratings made their way into these pages without any editorial changes to the list. The numbers spoke, and we obeyed.

You may think that some schools are conspicuously absent from this list and that others don't belong in it, but we stand by our selection. The selectivity rating indicates the colleges to which the smartest, strongest high school students in America decided to apply, those colleges accepting them, and where these top-notch students ultimately enrolled. There are various reasons why the best students in the nation apply to and enroll in a select few colleges year after year. Whatever those unquantifiable qualities are that attract these students are what lead us to deem the following colleges elite.

Amherst College

Campus Box 2231, PO Box 5000, Amherst, MA 01002

Academics

Small classes, great professors, as much academic freedom as students are willing to grab, and a beautiful campus; no wonder students say, "I could not, in my wildest dreams, imagine an environment better suited for a young adult to grow intellectually than Amherst

Selectivity Rating	98
Undergraduate Enrollment	1,682
Average SAT Verbal	702
Middle 50% SAT Verbal	650–760
Average SAT Math	696
Middle 50% SAT Math	650–740
Average ACT	30
Middle 50% ACT	28–32
% Graduating in Top 10% of Class	84

College." Excellent professors dedicated to undergraduate teaching lie at the heart of the Amherst experience. "Professors make it their business to get to know students and show an interest in them," writes one undergrad. "They are very supportive." Recounts another, "When I wrote my math professor a panic-filled e-mail the night before a test, he called me to help at one in the morning." The administration aggressively encourages close student-teacher relationships, sponsoring "a program [that allows] students to take professors out to dinner and thus extend the educational realm beyond the classroom." Amherst's open curriculum means students "take every course by choice, not because it is required" and can easily "create [their] own interdisciplinary major." Classes are small and selection is limited, so classes close quickly. However, "while on paper it may seem [difficult] to get into classes, Amherst students take the words 'course closed' as a challenge. Here, the administration and many professors encourage us to whine and grovel to get what we want out of our academics. The rules are written so that anyone can be an exception." When students tire of their own college community, it is easy to take a class or audition for a play at one of the other four schools in the Five College Consortium (UMass—Amherst, Smith, Hampshire, and Mount Holyoke). The Five College system, according to students, "gives you all the opportunities of a large university, without any of the drawbacks."

Admissions Phone: 413-542-2328 • Fax: 413-542-2040 •
Financial Aid Phone: 413-542-2296 • E-Mail: admissions@amherst.edu •
Website: www.amherst.edu

The Inside Word

Despite an up-and-down fluctuation in application totals at most highly selective colleges over the past couple of years, Amherst remains a popular choice and very competitive. You've got to be a strong match all-around, and given their formidable applicant pool, it's very important that you make your case as direct as possible. If you're a special-interest candidate such as a legacy or recruited athlete, you may get a bit of a break from the admissions committee, but you'll still need to show sound academic capabilities and potential. Those without such links have a tougher task. On top of taking the toughest courses available to them and performing at the highest of their abilities, they must be strong writers who demonstrate that they are intellectually curious self-starters who will contribute to the community and profit from the experience. In other words, you've got to have a strong profile and a very convincing application in order to get admitted.

FROM THE ADMISSIONS OFFICE

"Amherst College looks, above all, for men and women of intellectual promise who have demonstrated qualities of mind and character that will enable them to take full advantage of the college's curriculum. . . . Admission decisions aim to select from among the many qualified applicants those possessing the intellectual talent, mental discipline, and imagination that will allow them most fully to benefit from the curriculum and contribute to the life of the college and society. Whatever the form of academic experience—lecture course, seminar, conference, studio, laboratory, independent study at various levels—intellectual competence and awareness of problems and methods are the goals of the Amherst program, rather than the direct preparation for a profession."

Bates College

23 Campus Avenue, Lewiston, ME 04240-9917

Academics

If you were to give us a nickel for every time a Bates College student tells us "this school is great; I just love it" or "I have had such a positive experience here" or something along those lines, we could probably stop updating

Selectivity Rating	97
Undergraduate Enrollment	1,694
Average SAT Verbal	660
Middle 50% SAT Verbal	620–710
Average SAT Math	670
Middle 50% SAT Math	630–700
% Graduating in Top 10% of Class	56

this book every year and retire to a nice island in the South Pacific. Bates is a "small, intimate" liberal arts college that follows a 4-4-1 calendar. There is a fall and a winter semester, then a "Short Term" in May that provides students with opportunities to study less traditional topics, or to study or intern off campus. Bates offers an academic atmosphere conducive to learning. "The faculty is fabulous," but "the work here is hard." The "dedicated and enthusiastic" professors here are notoriously difficult graders, and all students must complete a thesis or a comprehensive exam in their major to graduate. "The thesis thing really blows," warns a senior, "but you do learn a lot." Administratively, Bates is the picture of stability—since 1855 they've had only six presidents and only two budgets in the red. When problems arise, the "professors and administrators are very approachable," according to a first-year student. "Whenever I need help I can usually count on it."

Admissions Phone: 207-786-6000 • Fax: 207-786-6025
Financial Aid Phone: 207-786-6060 • E-Mail: admissions@bates.edu •
Website: www.bates.edu

The Inside Word

With or without test scores, the admissions office here will weed out weak students showing little or no intellectual curiosity. Students with high SAT scores should always submit them. If you are curious about Bates, it is important to have solid grades in challenging courses; without them, you are not a viable candidate for admission. Tough competition for students between the College and its New England peers has intensified greatly over the past couple of years; Bates is holding its own. It remains a top choice among its applicants, and as a result selectivity is on the rise.

FROM THE ADMISSIONS OFFICE

"The people on the Bates admissions staff read your applications carefully several times. We get to know you from that reading. Your high school record and the quality of your writing are particularly important. We strongly encourage a personal interview, either on campus or with an alumni representative.

"When you come to Bates, you will see how Bates students benefit greatly from being in Maine. Many internship possibilities exist here in the sciences and social sciences for people who want to try out different fields.

"Visit our website, www.bates.edu, to learn more about living and learning here."

Brown University

Box 1876, 45 Prospect Street, Providence, RI 02912

Academics

The current trend in undergraduate education is toward more structured curricula and increased requirements for graduation. In this regard—and perhaps only in this regard—popular Brown University remains defiantly unfashionable. Brown's New Curriculum imposes no course

Selectivity Rating	98
Undergraduate Enrollment	6,029
Average SAT Verbal	690
Middle 50% SAT Verbal	640–750
Average SAT Math	690
Middle 50% SAT Math	650–740
Average ACT	29
Middle 50% ACT	27–32
% Graduating in Top 10% of Class	87

requirements on undergrads. Furthermore, it includes an unusually lenient grading system that allows students to choose between ABC/No Credit (wherein grades below C do not appear on students' transcripts) and Pass/No Credit (essentially Pass/Fail without the Fail option). Writes one student, "Brown is definitely the school for those who want an active role in their education. Students are given an immense amount of freedom and there are amazing resources and teachers at one's disposal. It does, however, take initiative on the students' part." One benefit of the system is that "students are self-driven, yet the academic atmosphere is relaxed. Competition between students is practically nonexistent." Some complain, however, that "the New Curriculum is a cop-out for professors to forego their responsibilities toward students. They never reach out until you fail." Despite the apparent laxity of Brown's policies, "This school is tough, but it's worth it. My teachers love students, teaching, and their field. My overall experience has been great. Every class can rock if you put in the effort. It's almost impossible to do all of the work for all of your classes, though. It's all about selective slacking for survival." Professors, who "are generally open and available outside of class," will make "incredible research opportunities" available to students who seek them out.

Admissions Phone: 401-863-2378 • Fax: 401-863-9300 •
Financial Aid Phone: 401-863-2721 •
E-Mail: admission_undergraduate@brown.edu • Website: www.brown.edu

The Inside Word

The cream of just about every crop applies to Brown. Gaining admission requires more than just a superior academic profile from high school. Some candidates, such as the sons and daughters of Brown graduates (who are admitted at virtually double the usual acceptance rate), have a better chance for admission than most others. Minority students benefit from some courtship, particularly once admitted. Ivies like to share the wealth and distribute offers of admission across a wide range of constituencies. Candidates from states that are overrepresented in the applicant pool, such as New York, have to be particularly distinguished in order to have the best chance at admission. So do those who attend high schools with many seniors applying to Brown, as it is rare for more than two or three students from any one school to be offered admission.

FROM THE ADMISSIONS OFFICE

"Brown University was founded in 1764 and is a private, coeducational, Ivy League university in which the intellectual development of undergraduate students is fostered by a dedicated faculty on a traditional New England campus. Brown is a university-college where the resources of a university are combined with the atmosphere of a liberal arts college, and where undergraduates are engaged in the design of their academic programs."

California Institute of Technology

1200 East California Boulevard, Pasadena, CA 91125

Academics

Students at the California Institute of Technology brag that their school offers "the best programs for science and technology in the country" and, unlike many similarly proud undergrads at other institutions, they may just

Selectivity Rating	98
Undergraduate Enrollment	929
Average SAT Verbal	727
Middle 50% SAT Verbal	690–780
Average SAT Math	776
Middle 50% SAT Math	760–800
% Graduating in Top 10% of Class	98

be right. Certainly Caltech boasts an impressive faculty, one that could allow a student to boast that he's "had lunch with no fewer than three Nobel laureates. People here are really accessible; you can pretty much wander into anyone's office." Access to all this brilliance, world-class facilities, and a "suicidal (yet effective) workload" constitute Caltech's formula for greatness. An excellent teaching faculty, alas, is not part of the equation. Professors "are great researchers and horrible teachers" who "give vaguely coherent lectures, then let us learn the material from the homework and tests." Instruction isn't uniformly obtuse: "Half the professors know the material too well to teach it, but the other half remember the joy of learning and care enough about their students to make every lecture worth waking up for at 8 a.m." Elaborates one student, "Typically, the CORE courses are poorly taught by very good professors. The professors in the upper-division classes are much better teachers, and the classes are smaller, which also helps." The workload at Caltech increases as the instruction improves; writes one student, "The freshman academic load is bearable, almost easy, but it gets harder every year. Students are encouraged to do homework in groups, which makes the most difficult homework sets much more bearable." The school works hard to help students deal with the academic pressure. First-year classes are Pass/Fail and "instead of strict rules and policies, people at Caltech follow an Honor Code. It gives students a lot of privileges such as take-home exams, collaboration on homework, and access to master keys."

Admissions Phone: 626-395-6341 • Fax: 626-683-3026
Financial Aid Phone: 626-395-6280 • E-Mail: ugadmissions@caltech.edu
Website: www.admissions.caltech.edu

The Inside Word

A mere glance at Caltech's freshman profile can discourage all but the most self-confident of high school seniors. It should. The impact of grades and test scores on the admissions process is minimized significantly when virtually every freshman was in the top fifth of his or her high school class and has a 1400 SAT. The admissions office isn't kidding when they emphasize the personal side o f their criteria. Six students are on the admissions committee; every file is read at least twice. The process is all about matchmaking, and the Tech staff is very interested in getting to know you. Don't apply unless you have more than high numbers to offer.

FROM THE ADMISSIONS OFFICE

"The California Institute of Technology, also known as Caltech, is a small, private, research university focused on math, science and engineering. The goal of Caltech is to educate students to become creative scientists and engineers who, as President Emeritus Everhart once said, 'look ahead and…dare to do the most ambitious things that human beings can accomplish.'

"With this goal in mind, admissions decisions are based on many factors. The most important criterion is the strength of academic preparation and potential. We look for dedicated scholars and curious thinkers who pursue intellectual challenges, and applicants are strongly encouraged to seek out and enroll in the most challenging courses available to them. We also look for students who will contribute to our close-knit campus community. More is not necessarily better with respect to activities; instead we are interested in a demonstration of initiative, sustained commitment, and leadership in the activities that are most important to our applicants. Since an interview is not part of the admissions process, essays and letters of recommendation are carefully reviewed and weighed heavily. Finally—and perhaps most importantly—we look for evidence of a passion for math, science or engineering, which will motivate and inspire students to take advantage of, and make contributions to, Caltech.

"Applications are evaluated by admissions officers and professors who review each application on an individual basis; we do not use any formulas, and we do not have minimum SAT or GPA requirements. If you have any questions about the admissions process or about Caltech in general, please call, write or e-mail us. We'd love to hear from you."

Columbia University

535 West 116th Street, New York, NY 10027

Academics

Columbia University holds one major trump card in its battle against Princeton, Yale, Dartmouth, and the other members of the Ivy League: location. Students agree that, among CU's many assets, New York City is tops. "I believe that

Selectivity Rating	98
Undergraduate Enrollment	13,464
Average SAT Verbal	701
Middle 50% SAT Verbal	650–760
Average SAT Math	693
Middle 50% SAT Math	650–740
% Graduating in Top 10% of Class	83

being in New York makes this the most well-rounded education anywhere," notes one student succinctly. Other drawing cards include world-class programs in engineering ("Engineering will challenge everything you know and believe in, every way you act, and absolutely every thought you have"), pre-medicine, pre-business, the liberal arts, and screenwriting. Then, of course, there's the much-vaunted core curriculum, a two-year sequence of survey courses in western culture. Enthuses one student, "The core curriculum changed my life. It taught me to love and appreciate the western canon, that it was mine to inherit." Another notes that the core, which most students complete by the end of sophomore year, sets the tone for all Columbia course work: "Columbia is all about discussion in its core curriculum and its discussion sections and seminars. Students who come here should be prepared to spar in debate in the classroom." They should also be prepared to fend for themselves, because "Columbia is a haven for the self-motivated. No one's going to hold your hand." Students "have to work and seek out the good professors, but if you put in the effort to find them, it's more than worth it." They also must prepare to do battle with "the brutal bureaucracy. . . . If you're not assertive and self-sufficient, it can be easy to get lost in the proverbial shuffle." Students agree that Columbia, like its hometown, is "a place that teaches you to sink or swim."

Admissions Phone: 212-854-2521 • Fax: 212-894-1209 •
Financial Aid Phone: 212-854-3711 • E-Mail: ugrad-admiss@columbia.edu •
Website: www.columbia.edu

The Inside Word

Columbia's application increases continue to outpace the rest of the Ivy League, and as a result the University keeps moving higher up in the Ivy pecking order. Crime is down in New York City, the football team wins (while still in baby-blue uniforms, no less!), and Columbia has become even more appealing. It's less selective than the absolute cream of the Ivy crop, but offers the advantage of being a bit more open and frank in discussing the admissions process with students, parents, and counselors—refreshing amid the typical shrouds of Ivy mystique.

FROM THE ADMISSIONS OFFICE

"Located in the world's most international city, Columbia University offers a diverse student body a solid and broad liberal arts curriculum foundation coupled with more advanced study in specific departments."

Cooper Union

30 Cooper Square, New York, NY 10003

Academics

Every student at the "prestigious" Cooper Union for the Advancement of Science and Art receives a full-tuition scholarship. The only catch is that students may only major in art, architecture, or engineering. It's an unbelievably good deal,

Selectivity Rating	99
Undergraduate Enrollment	870
Average SAT Verbal	680
Middle 50% SAT Verbal	600–720
Average SAT Math	700
Middle 50% SAT Math	670–740
Average High School GPA	3.2
% Graduating in Top 10% of Class	80

considering Cooper's "incredible reputation" as "the best engineering undergraduate school on the East Coast." Students praise the "rigorous" and "unparalleled academics" here, though the process sometimes resembles "boot camp," and there is a meager allotment of good grades. "Unless you are a genius or super-lucky, you've got to work really hard to do well," discloses a junior. "So many of us try so hard to just do okay in our classes." Some of the "acclaimed" and "very dedicated" professors at Cooper are "the best in the city." They "challenge the students" and make themselves "very accessible outside of class." However, a good chunk of the faculty is merely "above average" and still others are "really awful." Though they are "extremely smart," some profs "just don't have what it takes to be good teachers." Also, many "don't understand how much work they assign and how much other teachers assign," suspects a chemical engineering major. Consequently, students spend endless hours in the library, and much of what they learn is apparently self-taught. "Whether they're good or bad, the professors are characters," according to a first-year student. They are "the kind of people it's fun to do impressions of." A "bit of a bureaucracy problem" notwithstanding, students have few complaints about the Cooper administration, as "students get the attention they need" and "interaction with administrators and deans is commonplace."

Admissions Phone: 212-353-4120 • Fax: 212-353-4342 •
Financial Aid Phone: 212-353-4130 • E-Mail: admissions@cooper.edu •
Website: www.cooper.edu

The Inside Word

It is ultra-tough to gain admission to Cooper Union, and will only get tougher. Loads of people apply here, and national publicity and the addition of dorms have brought even more candidates to the pool. Not only do students need to have top academic accomplishments but they also need to be a good fit for Cooper's offbeat milieu.

FROM THE ADMISSIONS OFFICE

"Each of the three schools, architecture, art, and engineering, adheres strongly to preparation for its profession and is committed to a problem-solving philosophy of education in a unique, scholarship environment. A rigorous curriculum and group projects reinforce this unique atmosphere in higher education and contribute to a strong sense of community and identity in each school. With McSorley's Ale House and the Joseph Papp Public Theater nearby, Cooper Union remains at the heart of the city's tradition of free speech, enlightenment, and entertainment. Cooper's Great Hall has hosted national leaders, from Abraham Lincoln to Booker T. Washington, from Mark Twain to Samuel Gompers, from Susan B. Anthony to Betty Friedan, and more recently, Bill Clinton."

Cornell University

410 Thurston Avenue, Ithaca, NY 14850

Academics

Ivy League member Cornell boasts a catalog of over 4,000 undergraduate courses, and a top notch faculty to boot. One student boasts "Profs are friendly and approachable." Classes at Cornell are a combination of lectures

Selectivity Rating	97
Undergraduate Enrollment	13,590
Average SAT Verbal	660
Middle 50% SAT Verbal	620–710
Average SAT Math	700
Middle 50% SAT Math	650–750
Average ACT	29
% Graduating in Top 10% of Class	82

and sections. Professors teach lectures, and TAs teach sections. And "it's always a pleasant surprise when a TA can speak English." Professor accessibility is also good; as one student notes, "most will give you their home number for extra assistance." Most students agree with this sentiment. The hotel school earns high marks from students. And while students have positive feelings about their professors, their opinion of the administration is nearly unanimous. Cornell is "not called 'The Big Red Tape' for nothing." Bear Access, Cornell's computer-based class registration system, "is a nightmare the day classes go open for registration." Switching courses is also a difficult process, and students who attempt to do so find themselves "run[ning] all over campus to accomplish anything." Students complain that the advising system is weak, and "advisors really have no idea what their advisees need to have accomplished for graduation." Supplemental costs are a major sticking point. "Cornell loves to charge fees for whatever it can—Internet, using the gym, buses, parking, cable, many gym classes, printing. You name it, it ain't free." "The general feeling at Cornell is that the undergrads pay for the grad students."

Admissions Phone: 607-255-5241 • Fax: 607-255-0659 •
Financial Aid Phone: 607-255-5145 • E-Mail: admissions@cornell.edu •
Website: www.cornell.edu

The Inside Word

Cornell is the largest of the Ivies, and its admissions operation is a reflection of the fairly grand scale of the institution: complex and somewhat intimidating. Candidates should not expect contact with admissions to reveal much in the way of helpful insights on the admissions process, as the university seems to prefer to keep things close to the vest. Only applicants with top accomplishments, academic or otherwise, will be viable candidates. The university is a very positive place for minorities, and the public status presents a value that's hard to beat.

FROM THE ADMISSIONS OFFICE

"The admissions process at Cornell University reflects the personality of the institution. When students apply to Cornell, they must apply to one of the seven undergraduate colleges. Applications are reviewed within each undergraduate college by individuals who know the college well. Life at Cornell is a blend of college-focused and University activities, and Cornell students participate at both the college and University level. Cornell students can take classes in any of the seven undergraduate colleges and they participate in one of the largest extracurricular/athletics programs in the Ivy League. Prospective students are encouraged to examine the range of opportunities, both academic and extracurricular, at Cornell. Within this great institution, there is a wealth of possibilities."

Dartmouth College

6016 McNutt Hall, Hanover, NH 03755

Academics

There are few schools in North America that can boast the combination of world-class academics and beautiful location that Dartmouth College offers its students. This Ivy-League institution, tucked away in Hanover, New

Selectivity Rating	98
Undergraduate Enrollment	4,057
Average SAT Verbal	708
Middle 50% SAT Verbal	660–760
Average SAT Math	713
Middle 50% SAT Math	670–760
Middle 50% ACT	29–33
% Graduating in Top 10% of Class	86

Hampshire, is the home of wonderful, caring professors, who are committed to the academic needs of their students. A sophomore German major speaks for the majority of students when he writes, "I love Dartmouth because it offers world-class professors who are there because they love to teach." Professors are always accessible, thanks to the Blitz—the campus Internet network—and many students note that they have been invited to their professors' houses for dinner. Students would like too see more study space on campus, though. While the professors are beloved, students don't feel quite the same way about the "draconian" administration. One student writes that the administration "thinks of this school as an advanced placement version of Disney World. You pay, and we hold your hand and kick you out when the park closes." A disheartened senior adds, "Dartmouth's administration has made every effort to destroy a wonderful school. They are attempting to turn Dartmouth into another cookie cutter example of a bland, lifeless university." A more glass-half-full type sophomore provides a little better marketing copy: "Dartmouth's academic experience is unbeatable because it unites a small liberal arts school with all the resources of a top university."

Admissions Phone: 603-646-2875 • Fax: 603-646-1216 •
Financial Aid Phone: 603-646-2451 • E-Mail: admissions.office@dartmouth.edu •
Website: www.dartmouth.edu

The Inside Word

Applications for the class of 2004 were down slightly less than 1 percent from the previous year's totals, but that certainly doesn't make this small-town Ivy any less selective in choosing who gets offered a coveted spot in the class. As is the case with those who apply to any of the Ivies or other highly selective colleges, candidates to Dartmouth are up against (or benefit from) many institutional interests that go unmentioned in discussions of appropriate qualifications for admission. This makes an already stressful process even more so for most candidates.

FROM THE ADMISSIONS OFFICE

"Dartmouth, the ninth oldest college in America and a member of the Ivy League, has a deeply rooted mission to endow its students with the knowledge and wisdom needed to make creative and positive contributions to society. Here, a breadth of ideas and cultures come together to create a campus that is alive with ongoing debate and exploration. From the extensive library system and modern laboratories to the world-class faculty, the College provides its students with everything they need to fully pursue their interests. Dartmouth's resources rival those of the finest large universities. At the same time and equally important, the College emphasizes individual learning experiences in the tradition of a small college. Dartmouth has an unswerving commitment to the undergraduate liberal arts experience. The College is large enough to support an extensive array of programs, yet intimate enough to promote the close interaction among students, administrators, and faculty that has created the special spirit and strong sense of community so evident on campus. The educational value of such interaction cannot be underestimated. From student-initiated roundtable discussions that attempt to make sense of world events to the late-night philosophizing in a residence hall lounge, Dartmouth students take advantage of their opportunities to learn from each other. The unique benefits of sharing in this discourse are accompanied by a great sense of responsibility. Each individual's commitment to the Principles of Community ensures the vitality of this learning environment."

Davidson College

PO Box 1737, Davidson, NC 28036-1719

Academics

Davidson undergrads overwhelmingly agree that, true to the school's reputation, "the workload is significant at Davidson. There is no such thing as an easy course here." Why would anyone choose a school knowing that "academics are intense, and the amount of work

Selectivity Rating	97
Undergraduate Enrollment	1,679
Average SAT Verbal	659
Middle 50% SAT Verbal	620–710
Average SAT Math	663
Middle 50% SAT Math	620–710
Average ACT	29
Middle 50% ACT	28–31
% Graduating in Top 10% of Class	75

assigned is often too cumbersome"? Explains one student, "The strong and brave of heart survive at Davidson. While about 50 percent of the people in the Southeast know about Davidson, it truly lives up to its reputation as the 'Princeton of the South.' The academics are rigorous, but the doors Davidson opens are worthwhile." Helping students cope with their difficult studies are an "administration and amazing faculty [who] strive to support every effort in and out of the classroom." Professors here "are eager to help you anytime. You can call them at home if you have any concerns or questions about the course." Notes one undergraduate, "Profs I've never met will introduce themselves in the hall because they heard of a paper I'm writing for another professor, and want to offer their help." Recounts another, "I never thought this would happen in college . . . but I walked by the president's office late one night. He was in there, and I stuck my head in and waved, and he called me in just to chat for about 20 minutes. I think that's a testament to the accessibility of administration and faculty here." Students also love the school's Honor Code, which allows for self-scheduled exams. Writes one student, "Most campuses have some version of the Honor Code, but it is rarely taken as seriously as it is here. I have yet to see any cheating, both because the students respect the code and because they are motivated to learn on their own."

Admissions Phone: 704-894-2230 • Fax: 704-894-2016 •
Financial Aid Phone: 704-892-2232 • E-Mail: admission@davidson.edu •
Website: www.davidson.edu

The Inside Word

Even though Davidson is little known outside the South, harbor no illusions regarding ease of admission. Getting in is every bit as tough as staying in, because an amazingly high percentage of those who are admitted choose to attend. Look for admission to become even more difficult as the college's name recognition increases.

FROM THE ADMISSIONS OFFICE

"Davidson College is one of the nation's premier academic institutions, a college of the liberal arts and sciences respected for its intellectual vigor, the high quality of its faculty and students, and the achievements of its alumni. It is distinguished by its strong honor system, close interaction between professors and students, an environment that encourages both intellectual growth and community service, and a commitment to international education. Davidson places great value on student participation in the life of the college. The college has a strong regional identity, which includes traditions of civility and mutual respect, and has historic ties to the Presbyterian Church.

"Davidson has long and justly prided itself on an educational mission that has yielded generation after generation of leaders, making leadership, character, and academic potential important criteria for admission. Financial circumstances have no bearing on admissions decisions, and the assurance that financial need will be met has been a cherished principle of college policy."

Duke University

2138 Campus Drive, Durham, NC 27708

Academics

There's no shortage of pride at Duke University, even when expressing criticism. Where else would a student complain that "the administration is trying to turn this place into Harvard, which it should not be, because as

Selectivity Rating	98
Undergraduate Enrollment	6,325
Middle 50% SAT Verbal	640–740
Middle 50% SAT Math	660–760
Average ACT	30
Middle 50% ACT	28–33
% Graduating in Top 10% of Class	86

we are now, this is a better place to go to college"? We seriously doubt that Duke administrators are trying to develop a tradition of rotten basketball (go Crimson!), but they are hard at work building an academic powerhouse that can hold its own against any other. Duke is one of the nation's most competitive universities; it boasts incredible resources, a beautiful campus, outstanding faculty, and an academic program that is rigorous but not backbreaking. "Duke strikes a great balance between superior academics and an active student life"; students here spend much less time at the books than their counterparts at many top colleges. At the undergraduate level, Duke has two divisions: Trinity College of Arts and Sciences and the School of Engineering. Political science, economics, history, and engineering are favorite majors at this largely pre-professional student body. Though Duke is a major research university with world-class graduate programs, students report that their professors are "brilliant teachers and not just researchers," "amazingly inspirational," and "wonderful if you take advantage of them." It's no exception for engineers: "It's really easy to meet with the assistant dean . . . really, really helpful." Many feel alienated from the central administration, describing it as "out of touch." About 40 percent of the students go on to grad school immediately after graduation.

Admissions Phone: 919-684-3214 • Fax: 919-681-8941 •
Financial Aid Phone: 919-684-6225 • E-Mail: undergrad-admissions@duke.edu •
Website: www.duke.edu

The Inside Word

The way in which Duke discusses its candidate-review process should be a basic model for all schools to use in their literature. Just about all highly selective admissions committees use rating systems similar to the one described above, but few are willing to publicly discuss them.

FROM THE ADMISSIONS OFFICE

"Duke University offers students a dynamic combination of tradition and innovation, a focus on undergraduate education with opportunities to participate in state-of-the-art research, friendliness and diversity throughout the university community, and intellectual vitality along with spirited athletic support. Students come to Duke from all over the United States and more than 80 foreign countries and represent a range of racial, ethnic, and socioeconomic backgrounds. They are in daily contact with world-renowned faculty members through small classes and independent study opportunities. More than 40 majors are available in engineering and the arts and sciences, and arts and sciences students may design their own curricula through Program II. Interdisciplinary certificate programs in several areas also are available. First-year students can participate in unique FOCUS programs, where students live and learn together, special first-year seminars, and courses taught in residence halls. All students are encouraged to study away from campus through approximately 120 study-abroad programs, as well as the Duke in New York and Duke in Los Angeles arts programs, the nearby Duke Primate Center, or the Duke Marine Laboratory located on the coast of North Carolina. While admission to Duke is highly selective, financial need is not a factor in the admissions decision for U.S. citizens and permanent residents, and the university pledges to meet 100 percent of the demonstrated financial need of all admitted students. The university also offers a limited number of merit and athletic scholarships."

Georgetown University

37th and P Streets NW, Washington, DC 20057

Academics

Georgetown University is the leader among the nation's 28 Jesuit colleges and universities. Undergrads study within four self-contained schools: Arts and Sciences, Business

Selectivity Rating	98
Undergraduate Enrollment	6,418
Middle 50% SAT Verbal	640–720
Middle 50% SAT Math	640–730
Middle 50% ACT	28–32
% Graduating in Top 10% of Class	78

Administration, Nursing, and the School of Foreign Service ("known worldwide"). No matter which of the schools you're in, get ready to hit the books ("We enjoy studying!"), because "Georgetown students work hard." Every student is required to take core requirements, including courses in the liberal arts and religious studies. "Georgetown is the best of a small school's atmosphere and a large school's opportunities (big-name professors and reputation)." The profs do indeed receive high grades from the students. One first-year student writes, "I am impressed by every teacher." Another adds, "It's nice to go to a school where professors are always being consulted by the media and politicians." She follows with a warning about celebrity faculty: "It is a rare occurrence to actually get [those] professors for a class." The few gripes the student body has about Georgetown are best put into perspective by one student's comment that "I couldn't be happier anywhere else, but I could be happier here." The bursar receives poor reviews; as one student told us, "The overall university administration is very bureaucratic and not student-friendly." "Classes should be easier for underclassmen to get into." But some students point out other positive aspects of the administration. "The deans are extremely accessible." Another big plus is abundant "internship opportunities, etc." to be found in the nation's capital. "More on-campus housing" would make many students happier. So would a more significant "commitment to the arts."

The Inside Word

It was always tough to get admitted to Georgetown, but in the early 1980s Patrick Ewing and the Hoyas created a basketball sensation that catapulted the place into position as one of the most selective universities in the nation. There has been no turning back since. GU gets almost 10 applications for every space in the entering class, and the academic strength of the pool is impressive. Virtually 50 percent of the entire student body took AP courses in high school. Candidates who are wait-listed here should hold little hope for an offer of admission; over the past several years Georgetown has taken very few off its lists.

FROM THE ADMISSIONS OFFICE

"Georgetown was founded in 1789 by John Carroll, who concurred with his contemporaries, Benjamin Franklin and Thomas Jefferson, in believing that the success of the young democracy depended upon an educated and virtuous citizenry. Carroll founded the school with the dynamic, Jesuit tradition of education, characterized by humanism and committed to the assumption of responsibility and action. Georgetown is a national and international university, enrolling students from all 50 states and over 100 foreign countries. Undergraduate students are enrolled in one of four undergraduate schools: the College of Arts and Sciences, School of Foreign Service, Georgetown School of Business, and Georgetown School of Nursing and Health Studies. All students share a common liberal arts core and have access to the entire university curriculum."

Harvard College

Byerly Hall, 8 Garden Street, Cambridge, MA 02318

Academics

Harvard College's "academic reputation" precedes it. Home to a distinguished faculty and phenomenal world-class research facilities, Harvard is the perhaps the most

Selectivity Rating	99
Undergraduate Enrollment	6,684
Middle 50% SAT Verbal	700–800
Middle 50% SAT Math	700–790
Middle 50% ACT	30–34
% Graduating in Top 10% of Class	90

prestigious hub of intellectual activity in America and is certainly one of the best academic universities on the planet. Students lucky and talented enough to gain admission have the opportunity to pursue virtually any academic interest under the tutelage of some of the finest minds ever. Not surprisingly, though, "there's not much hand-holding here," as the "really challenging" professors are the college faculty equivalent of rock stars. Harvard profs are, however, "more approachable than some people think." "One of my professors took Polaroids of his 200-person lecture so that he could learn our names," reports an awed sophomore. "We all thought it was great until he started cold-calling us in lecture by name." And another professor "gives milk and cookies to students who come to his office hours." There are, however, a considerable number of TAs who teach undergraduate courses, a situation that causes students to give the faculty only average marks. Overall, the administration runs Harvard College like butter.

Admissions Phone: 617-495-1551 • Fax: 617-495-8821 •
Financial Aid Phone: 617-495-1581 • E-Mail: college@fas.harvard.edu •
Website: www.fas.harvard.edu

The Inside Word

It just doesn't get any tougher than this. Candidates to Harvard face dual obstacles—an awe-inspiring applicant pool and, as a result, admissions standards that defy explanation in quantifiable terms. Harvard denies admission to the vast majority, and virtually all of them are top students. It all boils down to splitting hairs, which is quite hard to explain and even harder for candidates to understand. Rather than being as detailed and direct as possible about the selection process and criteria, Harvard keeps things close to the vest—before, during, and after. They even refuse to admit that being from South Dakota is an advantage. Thus the admissions process does more to intimidate candidates than to empower them. Moving to a common application seemed to be a small step in the right direction, but with the current explosion of early decision applicants and a super-high yield of enrollees, things are not likely to change dramatically.

FROM THE ADMISSIONS OFFICE

"The admissions committee looks for energy, ambition, and the capacity to make the most of opportunities. Academic ability and preparation are important, and so is intellectual curiosity—but many of the strongest applicants have significant nonacademic interests and accomplishments as well. There is no formula for admission and applicants are considered carefully, with attention to future promise."

Haverford College

370 Lancaster Avenue, Haverford, PA 19041

Academics

Selectivity Rating	97
Undergraduate Enrollment	1,135
Middle 50% SAT Verbal	630–730
Middle 50% SAT Math	630–720
% Graduating in Top 10% of Class	83

At prestigious Haverford College, a small school with a big reputation in the liberal arts and premedical sciences, "The professors aren't concerned with teaching you to think like the renowned critics and authors that we read in class. Instead, they teach us to think for ourselves." This approach is just one of the reasons why students remain steadfastly devoted to this school despite the backbreaking workload it often heaps upon them. Warns one psychology major, "Sometimes the amount of work makes us feel as though we're being hit by a tsunami. At least we know that we're all in the same boat." Other reasons include a faculty that is "amazing—passionate, accommodating, and extremely dedicated," and a much-loved, student-enforced Honor Code that governs not only academic activity but social activity as well. Explains one student, "The Honor Code affects so many aspects of academics and relationships. The Quaker heritage is prevalent here." Says another, "Picture yourself during finals week. Your professor hands you your test. You go to the library, put a blanket on your shoulders, take the test, and return it at your convenience. This is the essential Haverford: learning for the sheer joy of it." Small classes also contribute to the air of conviviality here; an academic partnership with Bryn Mawr College, which allows students to cross-register for courses and provides each campus access to the others' libraries, helps to mitigate the shortcomings of Haverford's small-school status.

Admissions Phone: 610-896-1350 • Fax: 610-896-1338 •
Financial Aid Phone: 610-896-1350 • E-Mail: admitme@haverford.edu •
Website: www.haverford.edu

The Inside Word

Candidate evaluation at Haverford is quite thorough, and the applicant pool is sizable and strong. Applicants who are successful through the initial academic review are then carefully considered for the match they make with the college. This part of the process is especially important at small schools like Haverford, and students should definitely spend some time assessing the reasons for their interest in attending before responding to essays and interviewing. Interviewing is a must.

FROM THE ADMISSIONS OFFICE

"Haverford strives to be a college in which integrity, honesty, and concern for others are dominant forces. The college does not have many formal rules; rather, it offers an opportunity for students to govern their affairs and conduct themselves with respect and concern for others. Each student is expected to adhere to the Honor Code as it is adopted each year by the Students' Association. Haverford's Quaker roots show most clearly in the relationship of faculty and students, in the emphasis on integrity, in the interaction of the individual and the community, and through the college's concern for the uses to which its students put their expanding knowledge. Haverford's 1,100 students represent a wide diversity of interests, backgrounds, and talents. They come from public, parochial, and independent schools across the United States, Puerto Rico, and 27 foreign countries. Students of color are an important part of the Haverford community. The Minority Coalition, which includes Asian, black, and Hispanic students' associations, works with faculty and administration on matters directly concerned with the quality of life at the college."

Johns Hopkins University

3400 North Charles Street/140 Garland, Baltimore, MD 21218

Academics

Prospective Johns Hopkins students, beware: A JHU education is not for the faint of heart. There's little of the hand-holding and kindly mentoring that characterizes small, undergrad-oriented colleges here. Students don't come to JHU for a warm, fuzzy experience,

Selectivity Rating	97
Undergraduate Enrollment	3,910
Average SAT Verbal	670
Middle 50% SAT Verbal	630–720
Average SAT Math	711
Middle 50% SAT Math	670–760
Average ACT	30
Middle 50% ACT	28–32
Average High School GPA	3.9
% Graduating in Top 10% of Class	70

though; they come for the prestige of graduating from one of the nation's top schools, one with a particularly stellar reputation in English, international studies, business, the sciences, and pre-medicine. Writes one student, "It's damn hard. But if it doesn't kill you, it will make you stronger." Says another, "Hopkins is a meat-grinder, but the post-graduate opportunities make it worth it. Hopkins has a strong alumni network that is a tremendous asset to students. Hopkins is much more than a pre-med mecca; the alumni network makes it especially valuable to anyone interested in business or Wall Street." Because of the school's focus on the sciences, "perhaps Hopkins' most valuable asset is its profound commitment to research, which paradoxically is also its most deplorable characteristic. A consequence of this commitment is that either top-notch researchers with abhorrent teaching skills, or else faculty who are completely uninterested in teaching students, are faced with the duty of engaging students in the material, with disastrous results." Agrees another student, "The science professors are rather wrapped up in their research, so [they] don't make office hours for students. Basically it's up to you and your book to learn the material. The liberal arts professors, however, are more enthusiastic about helping their students." Making the JHU experience more arduous still is a "big-school bureaucracy surrounded by small-school facilities." All the same, most agree that "there is a tremendous upside to attending JHU, so long as you are willing to actively pursue your interests."

Admissions Phone: 410-516-8171 • Fax: 410-516-6025 •
Financial Aid Phone: 410-516-8028 • E-Mail: gotojhu@jhu.edu •
Website: www.jhu.edu

The Inside Word

The admissions process at Hopkins demands to be taken seriously. Competition with the best colleges and universities in the country keeps the acceptance rate artificially high. Make certain that your personal credentials— essays, recommendations, and extracurricular activities—are impressive.

FROM THE ADMISSIONS OFFICE

"Admission to Johns Hopkins is extremely competitive. We have about 1,000 spaces available each year for which we receive almost 10,000 applications. However, we have no formula for decision-making; what we are looking for cannot be summarized in test scores or checklists. Hopkins was the first university in America to make original research the cornerstone of its academic programs, and students who succeed here learn how to express their brilliance and originality in unexpected ways. Identifying such students goes beyond any single set of criteria.

"We start with the usual quantitative and qualitative measures: academic courses, essays, recommendations, extracurricular interests, GPA, and test scores. We also look for more. Does your application express serious interest, a desire to contribute? Are you a good fit? We read carefully, searching for the answers. Individual interviews, overnight visits with current students, open houses, high school visits, and off-site receptions also help us decide if we are right for each other. If you are seriously considering Hopkins, get to know us. Make an effort to communicate. Better yet, visit us at our 140-acre, wooded and vibrant campus in one of Baltimore's safest and most beautiful neighborhoods.

"In terms of numbers, we are a small school. In terms of global impact, we are a major university. That means that each new student must aim for something great. Communicate that desire to us, and we will feed your ambitions and help you succeed. If you really want to come here, make sure your application tells us why."

Massachusetts Institute of Technology

77 Massachusetts Avenue, Cambridge, MA 02139

Academics

How intense is an MIT education? "Say you like Pez candy," posits one MIT undergrad. "MIT, then, is like being forced to eat 13,109 Pez candies." Indeed, "the workload is heavy" here, but the crunch is mitigated by an atmosphere of teamwork and a sense that students

Selectivity Rating	99
Undergraduate Enrollment	4,300
Average SAT Verbal	702
Middle 50% SAT Verbal	660–760
Average SAT Math	752
Middle 50% SAT Math	730–800
Average ACT	31
Middle 50% ACT	30–33
% Graduating in Top 10% of Class	94

are getting the very best education money can buy. They study directly under "Nobel Prize–winning faculty, even as freshmen" and enjoy access to "superior labs and outstanding opportunities for undergraduate research." Time management, students point out, is critical. "Tech is hell if you want to attend every lecture, read everything twice, do the homework perfectly, and ace every test," explains one student. "If you understand what does and does not help you learn, life here becomes much more manageable." Material "is taught extremely fast. It takes a few weeks to get used to, but it makes everything so much more interesting and motivating." Most classes consist of "lectures taught by a full professor and recitations taught by TAs." According to several students, "Usually, recitations by undergraduate and graduate TAs, not the classes taught by distinguished faculty, are the most helpful [in learning] the material." MIT's "world-renowned" profs are, for the most part, "excellent teachers as well as researchers. Some are not good at teaching. Many are famous and offer cutting-edge information." Students appreciate the fact that "freshman year is pass/no record, and that was awesome in helping me adjust," and also that "the administration has gone through a lot of work sorting us out and choosing whom to select. They really hate to see students flunk out or transfer."

Admissions Phone: 617-253-4791 • Fax: 617-253-1986 •
Financial Aid Phone: 617-253-4971 • E-Mail: admissions@mit.edu •
Website: www.mit.edu

The Inside Word

High academic achievement, lofty test scores, and the most rigorous high school courseload possible are prerequisites for a successful candidacy. Among the most selective institutions in the country, MIT's admissions operation is easily one of the most down-to-earth and accessible. Over the years they have shown both a sense of humor in admissions literature and an awareness that applying to such a prestigious and demanding place creates a high level of anxiety in students. Their relaxed and helpful approach does much to temper such stress.

FROM THE ADMISSIONS OFFICE

"The students who come to the Massachusetts Institute of Technology are some of America's—and the world's—best and most creative. As graduates, they leave here to make real contributions—in science, technology, business, education, politics, architecture, and the arts. From any class, a handful will go on to do work that is historically significant. These young men and women are leaders, achievers, producers. Helping such students make the most of their talents and dreams would challenge any educational institution. MIT gives them its best advantages: a world-class faculty, unparalleled facilities, remarkable opportunities. In turn, these students help to make the Institute the vital place it is. They bring fresh viewpoints to faculty research: More than three-quarters participate in the Undergraduate Research Opportunities Program. They play on MIT's 41 intercollegiate teams as well as in nearly 50 music, theater, and dance groups. To their classes and to their out-of-class activities, they bring enthusiasm, energy, and individual style."

Middlebury College

The Emma Willard House, Middlebury, VT 05753-6002

Academics

Academically one of the most rigorous programs in the country, "top-rate" Middlebury College, tucked away in rural Vermont (about four hours' drive to Boston, two hours to Burlington) manages to offer the resources, facilities, and faculty excellence of a much

Selectivity Rating	97
Undergraduate Enrollment	2,292
Average SAT Verbal	710
Middle 50% SAT Verbal	680–730
Average SAT Math	700
Middle 50% SAT Math	670–740
Average ACT	30
Middle 50% ACT	29–32
% Graduating in Top 10% of Class	73

larger school—while keeping enrollment for undergrads at around 2,300. Nationally recognized language, writing, and theater programs share the spotlight with a top-notch science curriculum—which has benefited in recent years from the construction of a new science center. One student is thrilled that "professors here actually teach. They manage classes, advising, and research demands seamlessly." Despite "tons of homework" and tough classes, students say there's little of the "cutthroat competition" that might characterize other schools of Middlebury's caliber. It might have something to do with the pristine location of "Club Midd," their "laid-back" atmosphere, and an excellent alumni network that makes finding a job after graduation a whole lot easier. Or it might be the result of a bit of grade inflation (some kids complain that "if you're smart, you can get A's and B's hardly doing any work"). But most likely, it's just Middlebury's special blend of a quality program, personal attention, and something a little more nebulous one student calls "attitude." In any case, Middlebury's got it. Sums up a senior, "Academically, I've been challenged, but also have had time to breathe and have fun."

Admissions Phone: 802-443-3000 • Fax: 802-443-2056 •
Financial Aid Phone: 802-443-5158 • E-Mail: admissions@middlebury.edu •
Website: www.middlebury.edu

The Inside Word

While Middlebury benefits tremendously from its age-old position as an Ivy League safety, it is nonetheless a very strong and demanding place in its own right. Middlebury has a broad national applicant pool and sees more ACT scores than most eastern colleges, so submitting ACT scores to Middlebury is a more comfortable option than at most eastern schools.

FROM THE ADMISSIONS OFFICE

"The successful Middlebury candidate excels in a variety of areas including academics, athletics, the arts, leadership, and service to others. These strengths and interests permit students to grow beyond their traditional 'comfort zones' and conventional limits. Our classrooms are as varied as the Green Mountains, the Metropolitan Museum of Art, or the great cities Russia and Japan. Outside the classroom, students informally interact with professors in activities such as intramural basketball games and community service. At Middlebury, students develop critical thinking skills, enduring bonds of friendship, and the ability to challenge themselves."

Northwestern University

PO Box 3060, 1801 Hinman Avenue, Evanston, IL 60208-3060

Academics

Considered by many an Ivy of the Midwest, Northwestern University is unarguably "an academically rigorous school" with an "awesome reputation" that "expects hard work from its students." Students warn that "academics here are very challenging, especially with the quarter system,"

Selectivity Rating	98
Undergraduate Enrollment	7,724
Average SAT Verbal	676
Middle 50% SAT Verbal	630–720
Average SAT Math	699
Middle 50% SAT Math	660–750
Average ACT	30
Middle 50% ACT	29–32
% Graduating in Top 10% of Class	84

which "makes the pace extremely hectic." Engineering, journalism, pre-medical studies, and the liberal arts departments are all well regarded, as is the "great theater program"—which, according to many, is "essentially a pre-professional program" that is uncommonly rigorous. Students caution that most of the professors here are among the "most important researchers in their fields" and that, while many are "genuinely interested in their students' performance" and "very generous with their time," others are "very research-oriented and lack teaching skills." During a given quarter, "it's likely that you'll take a class with the most enthusiastic and interesting person you've ever met and also one with a professor far inferior to your worst high school teacher." Fortunately, "the teacher evaluation information is excellent. There are so many classes to take here. Like anywhere, there are good and bad professors, but the evaluation system makes it easy to differentiate between them, and it's all online."

The Inside Word

Northwestern's applicant pool is easily among the best in the country. Candidates face both a rigorous evaluation by the admissions committee and serious competition from within the pool. The best approach (besides top grades and a strong personal background) is to take the committee up on their recommendations to visit the campus or interview with an alumnus/a and submit SAT II scores. The effort it takes to get in is well worth it.

FROM THE ADMISSIONS OFFICE

"Northwestern University is an ambitious institution, pushing to a level of preeminence achieved by only a handful of institutions in the world. It has distinguished itself as an institution that encourages innovation and the integration of experience across many fields. This culture positions Northwestern to lead higher education in the 21st century. Northwestern combines innovative teaching and pioneering research in a highly collaborative environment that transcends traditional academic boundaries. It provides students and faculty exceptional opportunities for intellectual, personal, and professional growth in a setting enhanced by the richness of Chicago. Northwestern offers an unusually broad range of substantive academic opportunities for an institution of its size. The combination of close interschool cooperation and a distinctive academic calendar enables students and faculty to individually tailor their education and research in innovative ways. Northwestern is a place where students at all levels learn from and do research with outstanding faculty and work with fellow students. It is an innovative and technologically sophisticated learning community in which students and faculty collaborate on academics and extracurricular activities. Northwestern University's emphasis on effective communication, regardless of field of study, fosters the ability to think analytically, write clearly, and speak persuasively. As a result, Northwestern University graduates are exceptionally well prepared for academic and professional success and become leaders in their fields. Northwestern University's location on Lake Michigan in Evanston and in the Chicago metropolitan area provide students and faculty a wealth of outstanding intellectual, professional, social, and cultural opportunities."

Princeton University

PO Box 430, Admission Office, Princeton, NJ 08544-0430

Academics

Princeton University is arguably the most undergraduate-friendly member of the Ivy League. Its peers and other institutions at a similar level of prestige often feature prominent and powerful professional schools in business, law, and/or medicine, but not

Selectivity Rating	99
Undergraduate Enrollment	4,663
Average SAT Verbal	740
Middle 50% SAT Verbal	700–780
Average SAT Math	750
Middle 50% SAT Math	710–790
Average ACT	33
Middle 50% ACT	31–35
% Graduating in Top 10% of Class	92

Princeton. Over the years, the students we've surveyed here are consistently among the nation's most satisfied with their overall academic experience. A sophomore sums it up as "my dream come true." Academic offerings are excellent; particularly noteworthy are engineering ("It has a friendly 'we're in this together' atmosphere—no 'cutthroat, kill-the-curve-breaker' competition like at MIT," writes one engineer), political science, history, religion, and English. Core distribution requirements guarantee that all students are schooled in the classic academic disciplines (math, natural and social sciences, humanities). A series of independent projects that culminates in a senior thesis gives upperclassmen an unusual amount of responsibility for their own education. "Precepts," once-a-week small-group discussion meetings with each class's professor or TA, offer the opportunity for more personal attention. Professors get solid reviews, ranging from the enthusiastic "brilliant," to the more down-to-earth "good and very accessible." TAs "deserve their much-maligned status" according to a sophomore, but a freshman opines that they're "often better teachers than professors." The amount of work here is "difficult but not overbearing"; Princeton students study no more than the average student surveyed for Best Colleges.

The Inside Word

Princeton is much more open about the admissions process than the rest of their Ivy compatriots. The admissions staff evaluates candidates' credentials using a 1–5 rating scale, common among highly selective colleges. In the initial screening of applicants, admissions staff members assigned to particular regions of the country eliminate weaker students before the admissions committee makes its evaluation. Princeton's recommendation to interview should be considered a requirement, given the ultra-competitive nature of the applicant pool. In addition, three SAT IIs are required; no joke, indeed.

FROM THE ADMISSIONS OFFICE

"Methods of instruction [at Princeton] vary widely, but common to all areas . . . is a strong emphasis on individual responsibility and the free interchange of ideas. This is displayed most notably in the wide use of preceptorials and seminars, in the provision of independent study for all upperclass students and qualified underclass students, and in the availability of a series of special programs to meet a range of individual interests. The undergraduate college encourages the student to be an independent seeker of information . . . and to assume responsibility for gaining both knowledge and judgment that will strengthen later contributions to society."

Rice University

PO Box 1892, Houston, TX 77251-1892

Academics

Justifiably promoted as the "Ivy of the South," Rice boasts a world-renowned faculty that actually enjoys teaching, state-of-the-art research facilities, a

Selectivity Rating	97
Undergraduate Enrollment	2,658
Middle 50% SAT Verbal	650–750
Middle 50% SAT Math	660–760
Middle 50% ACT	28–33

rigorous curriculum, and a student body that is up to the challenge. And, through the good graces of a massive endowment, Rice University is also one of the most affordable top-tier undergraduate programs in the country. Students here know how good they have it. Writes one, "Rice provides an intense academic atmosphere that revived the love of learning that high school had sucked out of me." Says another, "My introductory honors chemistry class is taught by a Nobel Prize winner in chemistry. Where else are freshmen taught by Nobel Prize winners?" Undergraduates must complete distribution requirements in the humanities, social sciences, and natural sciences along with all the requirements of their majors. A small student body means that "we always get the classes we want. It's the best thing about Rice." It also provides students with a voice in running the school. As one student tells us, "The administration and professors here are very receptive to the needs and wants of the students." An honor code affords students flexibility; explains one, "Because of the honor code, most professors are helpful in situations that come up when you can't make it to a test." No wonder students tell us "I made one of the best decisions in coming to Rice. The school gives students the opportunity to experiment and try new things with the safety net of a great support system."

Admissions Phone: 713-348-7423 • Fax: 713-348-5952 •
Financial Aid Phone: 713-348-4958 • E-Mail: admission@rice.edu •
Website: www.rice.edu

The Inside Word

Rice has gotten loads of positive publicity over the past few years. As a result, what was already an extremely selective university is even more so. Candidates with less than the most impressive applications are not likely to last long in the admissions process.

FROM THE ADMISSIONS OFFICE

"Admissions committee decisions are based not only on high school grades and test scores but also on such qualities as leadership, participation in extracurricular activities, and personal creativity. Admission is extremely competitive; Rice attempts to seek out and identify those students who have demonstrated exceptional ability and the potential for personal and intellectual growth."

Stanford University

520 Lasuen Mall, Old Union 232, Stanford, CA 94305-3005

Academics

There are perhaps a half-dozen universities in the United States with de facto Ivy League status. Though not actually members of the vaunted Ivy League, these schools are recognized as equal in stature to Dartmouth, Princeton, and Yale; without question, Stanford University is among this elite group.

Selectivity Rating	98
Undergraduate Enrollment	7,886
Average SAT Verbal	715
Middle 50% SAT Verbal	670–770
Average SAT Math	717
Middle 50% SAT Math	690–790
Average ACT	31
Middle 50% ACT	29–33
Average High School GPA	3.9
% Graduating in Top 10% of Class	89

Stanford students, however, enjoy several perks unknown to Ivy undergrads: a nationally ranked intercollegiate athletic program, an "almost carefree" atmosphere, and the truly hospitable California climate. Engineering, biology, physical science, and liberal arts programs are standouts among the uniformly strong academic disciplines here. Entering students encounter a mix of crowded required lecture classes ("You've got to be brave or a brown-noser to get to know your freshman-year profs," writes one student) and small seminars (through the recently added Freshman Seminars series), all of which rush by due to the quarterly academic schedule. Beyond freshman year, "the upper-division profs are more accessible and interested in getting to know you." Students tell us that "teaching is generally good" but deride the administration as "very image-oriented and politically conservative" and decry its fondness for "lots of bureaucracy and red tape." Overall, however, students are pleased with the academic experience here. Says one student, "You get what you pay (a lot) for."

The Inside Word

Not only is Stanford a pinnacle of academic excellence, but among the nation's ultra-selective universities it is one of the most compassionate toward students, both those who attend and those who aspire to attend. It isn't easy for an admissions staff to be warm and caring when your reputation is based in part on how many candidates you say "no" to. In our opinion, Stanford is the best of the best in this regard. Students who haven't devoted themselves to excellence in the same fashion that Stanford itself has are not likely to meet with success in gaining admission.

FROM THE ADMISSIONS OFFICE

"Stanford University is an independent, coeducational, nondenominational, residential institution with goals of practicality, humanism, and excellence. It provides students an abundant and challenging environment and much personal and academic freedom. Located in a residential area 40 minutes from San Francisco and the Pacific and four hours from the Sierra, Stanford's 8,800 acres consist of a central cluster of academic and residence buildings surrounded by rolling foothills and open space. The setting promotes an informal atmosphere and encourages use of the extensive academic, athletic, and fine arts facilities, which include an 85,000-seat football stadium, golf course, riding stables, an intimate theater, and one of the largest Rodin sculpture collections in the United States. Academic facilities and features include a faculty of 1,600, more than 60 majors, many interdepartmental and innovative programs, advanced scientific equipment, a network of 25 libraries, plus the opportunity for all students to study at one of the nine Overseas Studies Centers."

Swarthmore College

500 College Avenue, Swarthmore, PA 19081

Academics

A Swarthmore education is definitely not for the weak of heart. Commenting on the legendary workload here, one undergrad explains: "At times I feel like I signed up for married life with the Marquis de Sade—work enjoys beating

Selectivity Rating	97
Undergraduate Enrollment	1,428
Average SAT Verbal	718
Middle 50% SAT Verbal	680–770
Average SAT Math	706
Middle 50% SAT Math	660–760
% Graduating in Top 10% of Class	88

me down every night. But then I remember that I've learned more in one class than in four years of high school, and that makes it all better." Concurs another, "First you think they [i.e., the faculty] are out to get you. Then you think they're out to get everybody. Finally you realize they're just too damned smart. And from there it's easy—try to be as smart as them. You won't succeed (well, you might) and if you don't, suddenly you realize you've learned more than you ever thought possible." To ease students' transition from high-school academics to the rigors of college, Swarthmore offers all first-semester courses on a pass-fail basis only. "Do not underestimate the value of taking your first semester pass-fail!" notes one student. "It's a great way to adjust." To further facilitate success, the faculty provides a substantial support network to the school's budding scholars. "One of my profs has four hours a day of office hours, sometimes including weekends," explains one undergrad. Says another, "My professors have always been more than willing to help me in my academic ventures, even if the project I am working on is not specifically for his/her class." The end result is a student body confident of and competent in its skills. Recounts one student, "Last week, no lie, one of my professors asked me to proofread her latest journal submission because she wanted to know if it was understandable to the world at large. By the time you're a senior, you start to feel like a colleague more than just a student."

Admissions Phone: 610-328-8300 • Fax: 610-328-8580 •
Financial Aid Phone: 610-328-8358 • E-Mail: admissions@swarthmore.edu •
Website: www.swarthmore.edu

The Inside Word

Swarthmore is as good as they come; among liberal arts colleges there is none better. Candidates face an admissions process that is appropriately demanding and thorough. Even the best qualified of students need to complete their applications with a meticulous approach—during candidate evaluation, serious competition is just another file away. Those who are fortunate enough to be offered admission usually have shown the committee that they have a high level of intellectual curiosity, self-confidence, and motivation.

FROM THE ADMISSIONS OFFICE

"Swarthmore seeks to help its students realize their fullest intellectual and personal potentials combined with a deep sense of ethical and social concern. The curriculum is designed to evoke the maximum development from each student with options for independent study, interdisciplinary work, off-campus study and flexible programming, with keen attention to the individual needs and goals of each student. The Swarthmore College Honors Program offers additional intensive seminar-style learning experiences and final evaluation by examiners from other colleges and universities.

"Nonsectarian since 1908, Swarthmore remains proud of its founding by members of the Society of Friends and continues to value Quaker principles of personal integrity, social justice and the peaceful settlement of disputes. Students are encouraged to seek and apply truth and to test whatever truth one believes one has found.

"A rich extracurricular program offers students the opportunity to develop non-academic interests, special talents or simply explore new activities. Athletics, performing arts, visual arts, publications, social and political activist groups, community service, religious and cultural organizations attract high participation from the students. As a residential college, Swarthmore encourages a strong sense of community where scholars learn cooperatively and participate actively in decisions affecting the community at large. Swarthmore graduates of emerge as moral leaders and thinkers in academia, law, medicine, government, business and the arts."

United States Air Force Academy

HQ USAFA/RRS, 2304 Cadet Drive, Suite 200, USAF Academy, CO 80840-5025

Academics

Selectivity Rating	99
Undergraduate Enrollment	4,325
Average SAT Verbal	625
Middle 50% SAT Verbal	590–670
Average SAT Math	652
Middle 50% SAT Math	610–690
Average High School GPA	3.8
% Graduating in Top 10% of Class	55

"It's not at every college that you can learn how to fight, eat, and fly all on top of academics," but that's the United States Air Force Academy in a nutshell. Every student here receives a full scholarship that includes tuition, room and board, health care, and a monthly living allowance. Cadets also enjoy leadership training that "is second to none," academics "comparable to the Ivy League with more hands-on experience," and a "challenging" physical program. Also, not surprisingly, USAFA is on the cutting edge of technology, which allows cadets access to wind tunnels, shock tubes, rocket engines, and all manner of nifty gadgetry. Classes are "very small," and USAFA's "great" (though often "dry") professors are "always available for extra instruction." Thanks to an "intense" core curriculum, "you have to take classes in every area, no matter what your major is." Some cadets say "it's quite a load, but you get a very well-rounded education," while others gripe that "the core kills you" because it requires "too many classes." Either way, "your schedule is pretty much mapped out for you," as a management major explains. "You're going to get all your classes, and you're going to graduate in four years." On the undeniably bright side, optional courses include soaring, parachuting, and basic flying. In addition to academics, students take great pride in USAFA's strict honor code and, to put it bluntly, "you get the living crap trained out of you" here. From the "strenuous" Basic Cadet Training (called "beast," it begins the summer before first year) to combat, survival, and "escape training" in subsequent summers, vacation time is rare. Immediately upon graduation, a "guaranteed good job" as an Air Force officer (or pilot or medical school) awaits every cadet.

Admissions Phone: 719-333-2520 • Fax: 719-333-3012 •
E-Mail: nr_webmail@usafa.af.mil • Website: www.usafa.af.mil

The Inside Word

Candidates to the service academies face some of America's most challenging admissions standards. Air Force is no exception in this regard. In addition to a very rigorous academic review, students must first win a nomination from their congressman and pass a demanding physical fitness exam. If you make it through, it's worth the hard work and effort—few students turn down an offer of admission and the chance to join the fold of an elite student body. Admit rates are among the nation's lowest annually.

FROM THE ADMISSIONS OFFICE

"The mission of the United States Air Force Academy is to inspire and develop outstanding young men and women to become Air Force officers with knowledge, character and discipline; motivated to lead the world's greatest aerospace force in service to the nation. To fulfill this mission, the Academy is committed to producing officers who have the knowledge, character, and motivation essential to leadership in the Air Force. The Academy is dedicated to adapting curriculum and philosophy to meet changing needs and responsibilities, thereby remaining a vital national institution that serves our country's needs. Please see our web site at www.usafa.edu/rr for more information about the Air Force Academy."

United States Coast Guard Academy

31 Mohegan Avenue, New London, CT 06320-8103

Academics

Looking for a "prestigious" place where students develop "sound bodies, stout hearts, and alert minds," and "a liking for the sea and its lore"? Look no further. The United States Coast Guard Academy is just the place, and it's also one of the best bargains in higher education. Each

Selectivity Rating	97
Undergraduate Enrollment	838
Average SAT Verbal	612
Middle 50% SAT Verbal	560–660
Average SAT Math	639
Middle 50% SAT Math	600–680
Average ACT	26
Middle 50% ACT	25–29
% Graduating in Top 10% of Class	45

cadet at USCGA receives a full scholarship complete with a monthly stipend for uniforms, a laptop, and other expenses. After four years, graduates must serve five years as officers in the Coast Guard. The "small classes" here are "very demanding" though some subject matter—like core class requirements in Nautical Science—borders on "vocational." Freshman year begins in July, when new cadets undergo six weeks of physical and military training, then spend a week learning about sailing on "America's Tall Ship," the *Barque Eagle*, a magnificant sailing vessel that serves as a seagoing classroom. Sophomore and junior summers mostly entail a slew of shipboard training. Seniors spend 10 weeks of the summer aboard Coast Guard cutters learning how to be deck watch and engineering officers. During the regular school year, "you choose a major" and "take the classes you are told to take." USCGA's "enthusiastic, caring, and devoted" professors are "very approachable" and "are professional officers. They know how to sail, drive boats, and arrest drug smugglers." However, some "are a little lacking in their ability to convey knowledge." Explains one cadet, "You will learn more about yourself" here "than you could at an 'ordinary' school, and you will accomplish things you never thought you could."

The Inside Word

Coast Guard is the service academy with the least amount of public recognition. Not that it's any easier to get admitted. Candidates must also go through the rigorous multistep admissions process (though no congressional nomination is required), and can fall short on any of these steps and meet with a roadblock to admission. Those who pass muster join a very proud, if somewhat under-recognized, student body virtually equal in accomplishment to those at the other academies.

FROM THE ADMISSIONS OFFICE

"Founded in 1876, the United States Coast Guard Academy has a proud tradition as one of the finest colleges in the country. When you've completed the four-year Bachelor of Science program, you're prepared professionally, physically and mentally for the great challenges of the future. You'll learn from inspiring teachers in small classes and train in some of the world's most sophisticated labs using equipment as advanced as anything at other top science colleges. You'll have a level of training that will make you stand out from the crowd. Unlike the other federal academies, there are no congressional appointments to our Academy. Acceptance is based solely on annual competition among top students across the nation. The competition evaluates high school performance and standardized test scores—over 95 percent of entering students are in the top 20 percent of their high school classes. Just as important is leadership potential and the desire to serve your fellow Americans. Our student body reflects the best of American youth— with all its potential and diversity."

United States Military Academy

600 Thayer Road, West Point, NY 10996-1797

Academics

"West Point is unique in many ways: a military institution, a first-class university, and a national landmark all rolled into one," explains one cadet. "Our motto is 'duty, honor, country,' and sometimes duty looms much larger than the rest. Life is hard here, but its difficulty makes it fulfilling." The

Selectivity Rating	99
Undergraduate Enrollment	4,216
Average SAT Verbal	627
Middle 50% SAT Verbal	570–670
Average SAT Math	641
Middle 50% SAT Math	590–680
Average ACT	28
Middle 50% ACT	26–30
Average High School GPA	3.7
% Graduating in Top 10% of Class	50

West Point approach—to cram as much activity into one day as humanly possible—is "very tough. Learn to prioritize. If you procrastinate, you die. Be ready not to sleep." Notes one student, "Academics are tough, but it's the fact that you have no time to study that makes it hard." Life is strictly regimented here, as one would expect. Writes one student, "West Point is similar to high school, at times almost too similar. We start at 7, stop for lunch at 12, and then continue until 3. Classes are small, which means every professor knows your name." For nearly all freshmen and sophomores, "There is no class choice. All classes are required." And even upperclassmen warn that "it's the military: You pick the major, they choose the classes." Fortunately for students, "the professors here, for the most part, are amazing. They understand how rigorous our life is and will tutor you personally every day for hours if you need it." Cadets are the first to admit that this school is not for everyone. "The school is focused toward military development and officership, so if you don't want to be in the Army, don't come!" warns one. Concludes another, "West Point is a machine that takes you in, chews you up, and spits you out—but somehow you are tremendously better person for it." Upon graduation, cadets are commissioned as Second Lieutenants in the U.S. Army and must serve a minimum of five years of active duty.

Admissions Phone: 914-938-4041 • Fax: 914-938-3021 •
Financial Aid Phone: 914-938-3516 • E-Mail: 8dad@exmail.usma.army.mil •
Website: www.usma.edu

The Inside Word

Students considering a candidacy at West Point need to hit the ground running in the second half of their junior year. Don't delay initiating the application and nomination processes; together they constitute a long, hard road that includes not one but several highly competitive elements. Successful candidates must demonstrate strength both academically and physically, be solid citizens and contributors to society, and show true fortitude and potential for leadership. Admissions processes at other top schools can seem like a cakewalk compared to this, but those who get a nomination and pass muster through the physical part of the process have made it through the hardest part.

FROM THE ADMISSIONS OFFICE

"The United States Military Academy (USMA) is renowned because of its historic and distinguished reputation as a military academy, and as a leading, progressive institution of higher education. Made legendary in books and movies produced over the years, the Academy's "Long Gray Line" of graduates includes some of our nation's most famous and influential men: Ulysses S. Grant, Robert E. Lee, Thomas "Stonewall" Jackson, George S. Patton, Omar Bradley, Douglas MacArthur, Dwight Eisenhower, and Norman Schwarzkopf. Because of this superb education and leadership experience, West Point graduates historically have been sought for high-level civilian and military leadership positions. Their numbers include twenty generations of Army officers numbering in the tens of thousands, two U.S. presidents, several ambassadors, state governors, legislators, judges, cabinet members, educators, astronauts, engineers, and corporate executives.

"Today, West Point continues to provide hundreds of young men and women the unique opportunity to develop physically, ethically, and intellectually while building a foundation for an exciting, challenging, and rewarding career as an Army officer in the service of our nation."

United States Naval Academy

117 Decatur Road, Annapolis, MD 21402

Academics

The U.S. Naval Academy offers a great education at a great price—it's free. Midshipmen have one of the "toughest academic programs around," yet the "outstanding" professors are "always willing and ready to help in every way

Selectivity Rating	99
Undergraduate Enrollment	4,172
Average SAT Verbal	637
Middle 50% SAT Verbal	600–680
Average SAT Math	667
Middle 50% SAT Math	620–700
% Graduating in Top 10% of Class	56

possible." Classes are small and are all taught by full-time military and civilian faculty members. "Tough but rewarding" is how one midshipman sums up his experience here. "If you've never been challenged by academics, get ready for a surprise." Midshipmen must handle a demanding courseload along with naval officer training, and academically they find that "it's a challenge to do well on top of all the military responsibilities." Facilities are absolutely state-of-the-art, and the administration, as might be expected, runs a tight, efficient ship. The innovative core curriculum balances technical and non-technical subjects and has received national acclaim: As one midshipman remarks, "This is the only place I know where history majors are required to take electrical engineering, calculus, and physics courses." All students, regardless of major, are awarded a Bachelor of Science degree upon graduation.

Admissions Phone: 410-293-4361 • Fax: 410-295-1815 •
E-Mail: webmail@gwmail.usna.com • Website: www.usna.edu

The Inside Word

It doesn't take a genius to recognize that getting admitted to Annapolis requires true strength of character; simply completing the arduous admissions process is an accomplishment worthy of remembrance. Those who have successful candidacies are strong, motivated students, and leaders in both school and community. Perseverance is an important character trait for anyone considering the life of a midshipman—the application process is only the beginning of a truly challenging and demanding experience.

FROM THE ADMISSIONS OFFICE

"The Naval Academy offers you a unique opportunity to associate with a broad cross-section of the country's finest young men and women. You will have the opportunity to pursue a four-year program that develops you mentally, morally, and physically as no civilian college can. As you might expect, this program is demanding, but the opportunities are limitless and more than worth the effort. To receive an appointment to the academy, you need four years of high school preparation to develop the strong academic, athletic, and extracurricular background required to compete successfully for admission. You should begin preparing in your freshman year and apply for admission at the end of your junior year. Selection for appointment to the academy comes as a result of a complete evaluation of your admissions package and completion of the nomination process. Complete admissions guidance may be found at www.usna.edu."

University of Notre Dame

220 Main Building, Notre Dame, IN 46556

Academics

Students at Notre Dame don't mince words when it comes to boasting about the education and experiences they've received at their beloved alma mater. Call it Irish Pride. A senior provides a perfect example: "Notre Dame, besides simply BEING college football, is

Selectivity Rating	98
Undergraduate Enrollment	8,038
Average SAT Verbal	660
Middle 50% SAT Verbal	620–710
Average SAT Math	681
Middle 50% SAT Math	650–720
Average ACT	31
Middle 50% ACT	29–32
% Graduating in Top 10% of Class	84

great academically. You are practically guaranteed a job when you leave as long as you kept your grades at decent levels through school. What's more, ND is able to attract not only some of the best students, but also the best teachers."What is it about Notre Dame that engenders such love and devotion? It's the holy trinity of "tradition, faith, and academics" that sets Notre Dame apart, argue undergrads, who also find comfort in ND's "strong sense of community" and "unparalleled school spirit." These last two—and an alumni network that's been called "the biggest fraternity in the world"—are what "make all this studying bearable," notes a sophomore. For the most part, undergrads praise Notre Dame's faculty, curriculum, and resources, noting that the school's strong emphasis on classical liberal arts courses such as theology and philosophy, its top-notch science program, as well as its honor code, exemplify ND's "commitment to instilling quality and character" in its students. Being a big research school, there are the usual complaints about TA's teaching classes (though an honors student points out that she's gotten "the cream of the crop"—"three heads of departments as teachers already, and I'm a freshman!"). This is balanced, however, by the sense that "people really care about you at Notre Dame. You're not another number, but rather, you're respected as an intelligent human. You're expected to treat others in the same way, which creates a wonderful atmosphere."

Admissions Phone: 219-631-7505 • Fax: 219-631-8865 •
Financial Aid Phone: 219-631-6436 • E-Mail: admissio.1@nd.edu •
Website: www.nd.edu

The Inside Word

For most candidates, getting admitted to Notre Dame is pretty tough. Legacies, however, face some of the most favorable admissions conditions to be found at any highly selective university. Unofficially, athletic talents seem to have some influence on the committee as well: An enormous percentage of the total student body holds at least one varsity letter from high school, and many were team captains. Perhaps it's merely coincidence, but even so, candidates who tap well into the Notre Dame persona are likeliest to succeed.

FROM THE ADMISSIONS OFFICE

"Notre Dame is a truly national university with a student body of 10,000 drawn from all 50 states and 87 foreign countries. Excellence in undergraduate teaching as well as groundbreaking research contributes to our being consistently ranked among the nation's top 25 universities. Notre Dame's distinctive Catholic heritage challenges students to integrate scholarship and faith. The First Year of Studies program provides special assistance to our students as they make the adjustment from high school to college. The first-year curriculum includes many core requirements, while allowing students to explore several areas of possible future study. Spirited traditions and personal responsibility are fostered within our tight-knit, residential community. More than 80 percent of our undergraduates participate in service activities. Notre Dame students also develop leadership skills through involvement in 200 student organizations, 26 varsity teams and dozens of intramural and recreational sports. Over a quarter of our students study abroad in 16 different countries—a higher percentage than any other major research university. Notre Dame prides itself on being an environment of teaching and learning that fosters the development of mind, body and spirit."

University of Pennsylvania

1 College Hall, Philadelphia, PA 19104

Academics

With continuing increases in its popularity with students over the past several years, Penn is clearly a hot ticket. One student explains, "I think Penn's greatest strength is that whatever you decide to major in, you'll find yourself in a strong department, most of which are [among] the best in the

Selectivity Rating	98
Undergraduate Enrollment	9,687
Average SAT Verbal	683
Middle 50% SAT Verbal	640–730
Average SAT Math	709
Middle 50% SAT Math	670–760
Average ACT	30
Middle 50% ACT	28–32
Average High School GPA	3.9
% Graduating in Top 10% of Class	92

country." Students generally agree that the education they receive behind the Ivy-covered walls of this competitive institution is top-notch, especially at the Wharton School. "Being in Wharton means I am getting a wonderful liberal arts education with a very serious focus in business—exactly what I need to enter the real professional world." Not to be overlooked is Penn's College of Arts and Science; history and psychology are also top major choices. Students rave about the variety of opportunities that are available to them at Penn: "The first day of my history class, I went up to my professor and asked if she needed a research assistant, and voila, I had a job." Another adds, "The opportunities are definitely here if you have the drive to take advantage of them." Some find the professors "not focused on the students" and "hard to reach," but past reports of impersonal treatment from profs seem to have ebbed. "Profs here are incredible. They are so accessible and most genuinely want to know their students." The administration receives less glowing compliments, but students are quick to acknowlege that they're trying, noting that they've "encountered red tape, but on the whole, the administration tries really hard to help you."

Admissions Phone: 215-898-7507 • Fax: 215-898-9670 •
Financial Aid Phone: 215-898-1988 • E-Mail: info@admissions.ugao.upenn.edu •
Website: www.upenn.edu

The Inside Word

After a small decline three cycles ago, applications are once again climbing at Penn—the fourth increase in five years. The competition in the applicant pool is formidable. Applicants can safely assume that they need to be one of the strongest students in their graduating class in order to be successful.

FROM THE ADMISSIONS OFFICE

"A Revolutionary Spirit"

"The nation's first university, the University of Pennsylvania had its beginnings in 1740, some thirty-six years before Thomas Jefferson, Benjamin Franklin (Penn's founder), and their fellow revolutionaries went public in Philadelphia with incendiary notions about life, liberty and the pursuit of happiness. Today, Penn continues in the spirit of the Founding Fathers, developing the intellectual, discussion-oriented seminars that comprise the majority of our course offerings, shaping innovative new courses of study, and allowing a remarkable degree of academic flexibility to its undergraduate students.

"Penn is situated on a green, tree-lined, 260-acre, urban campus, four blocks west of the Schuylkill River in Philadelphia. The broad lawns that connect Penn's stately halls embody a philosophy of academic freedom within our undergraduate schools. Newly developed interdisciplinary programs fusing classical disciplines with practical, professional options enable Penn to define cutting-edge academia in and out of the classroom. Students are encouraged to partake in study and research that may extend into many of the graduate and professional schools. As part of our College House system, Penn's Faculty Masters engage students in academic and civic experience while leading residential programs that promote an environment where living and learning intersect around the clock.

"Penn students are part of a dynamic community that includes a traditional campus, a lively neighborhood, and a city rich in culture and diversity. Whether your interests include artistic performance, community involvement, student government, athletics, fraternities and sororities, or cultural and religious organizations, you'll find many different options. Most importantly, students at Penn find that their lives in and out of the classroom compliment each other and are full, interesting and busy.

"We invite you to visit Penn in Philadelphia. You'll enjoy the revolutionary spirit of the campus and city."

Washington and Lee University

Letcher Avenue, Lexington, VA 24450-0303

Academics

While not the best-known small, traditional, liberal arts school on the East Coast, Washington and Lee may well be the best loved by its students. The school is not for everyone—see Student Body, below—but for those who fit the mold,

Selectivity Rating	97
Undergraduate Enrollment	1,740
Middle 50% SAT Verbal	630–720
Middle 50% SAT Math	640–710
Middle 50% ACT	28–31
Average High School GPA	3.9
% Graduating in Top 10% of Class	74

W&L is a "little utopian society" that offers "really small classes" and a "strong sense of community among the students, faculty, and administration." These factors help mitigate the heavy workload here. Writes one student, "Academically, W&L is very challenging, but the small classes and group discussions make it very easy to participate and learn." Students say the faculty is "extremely helpful and always accessible" and appreciate professors who "epitomize southern hospitality. They're amazing!" All classes are taught by full professors; W&L has "no TAs, which is excellent." Undergrads are equally sanguine about the administration, reporting that the "administration and departments bend over backwards to help you out. If you are serious about learning and not just willing but want to work for your education, W&L will present excellent opportunities." The school runs on an unusual academic schedule, featuring two full-length terms (fall and winter) and a mandatory six-week term in the spring, during which students participate in seminars and internships or travel abroad. W&L also has a very popular Honor System that allows students to schedule their own nonproctored exams and leave their dorm rooms unlocked. Take-home, closed-book examinations are not uncommon, and "the buildings are open 24/7" as well. Brags one student, "The Honor System dominates life on campus and is a large part of what makes this university so special."

Admissions Phone: 540-463-8710 • Fax: 540-463-8062 •
Financial Aid Phone: 540-463-8715 • E-Mail: admissions@wlu.edu •
Website: www.wlu.edu

The Inside Word

If you're looking for a bastion of southern tradition, Washington and Lee is one of the foremost. Its admissions process is appropriately traditional, and highly selective. Under these circumstances, it is always best to take a cautious and conservative approach to preparing your candidacy. Smart applicants have taken the toughest courses available to them in high school—the minimum requirements aren't likely to help you gain admission. Neither will a glib approach to the personal side of the application; a well-written essay is what they're after.

FROM THE ADMISSIONS OFFICE

"W&L, the nation's eighth oldest college, is a small, private, liberal arts school located in the heart of the beautiful Shenandoah Valley. As one might expect, W&L possesses an inordinate amount of history. Quality teaching both in and out of the classroom and the development of students into well-rounded leaders, summarize the school's primary goals. An average W&L class contains 15 students, and courses are taught by the school's full-time faculty members; no graduate students or teacher assistants are on the faculty. W&L possesses a uniquely broad and deep curriculum as well as a time-honored, student-run Honor System that allows students a wide range of freedoms. W&L is a highly competitive school where students will receive a first-rate, personalized education, develop leadership skills, enjoy life outside of the classroom, and reap the innumerable postgraduation benefits of a W&L education."

Wellesley College

Board of Admission, 106 Central Street, Wellesley, MA 02481-8203

Academics

Wellesley, an all-women's undergraduate institution near Boston, is not just a college; it is also, according to one typical enthusiast, "a community dedicated to developing women of superior intellect, life skills, and savvy. It's simply the best. Wellesley has shown me that it is okay to be a

Selectivity Rating	97
Undergraduate Enrollment	2,287
Average SAT Verbal	685
Middle 50% SAT Verbal	640–730
Average SAT Math	670
Middle 50% SAT Math	630–710
Average ACT	29
Middle 50% ACT	27–31
% Graduating in Top 10% of Class	67

fabulous woman with so much to offer." Most students here simply can't decide what they like most about the school. It could be that classes "are small and well taught. There's good atmosphere for discussion in and out of the classroom." Or, it might be that students have "access to some of the best lecturers and facilities in the world. World-renowned experts give presentations here." Most likely, though, it's the professors. They "are Wellesley's gold. They give individual attention and that's why I'm here," writes one student. Another explains, "The professors are very knowledgeable but also very approachable. It's obvious they love teaching." Faculty and students "are very fond of each other—but not in a way that could get anyone fired." Students probably are less enthusiastic about the brutal workload the school demands, although most accept it as an essential part of the Wellesley experience. "It'll be the hardest four years of your life, but also the most rewarding," sums up one student.

Admissions Phone: 781-283-2270 • Fax: 781-283-3678 •
Financial Aid Phone: 781-283-2360 • E-Mail: admission@wellesley.edu •
Website: www.wellesley.edu

The Inside Word

While the majority of women's colleges have gone coed or even closed over the past two decades, Wellesley has continued with vigor. As a surviving member of the Seven Sisters, the nation's most prestigious women's colleges, Wellesley enjoys even more popularity with students who choose the single-sex option. Admissions standards are rigorous, but among institutions of such high reputation Wellesley's admissions staff is friendlier and more open than the majority. Their willingness to conduct preliminary evaluations for candidates is especially commendable and in some form or another should be the rule rather than an exception at highly selective colleges.

FROM THE ADMISSIONS OFFICE

"A student's years at Wellesley are the beginning—not the end—of an education. A Wellesley College degree signifies not that the graduate has memorized certain blocks of material, but that she has acquired the curiosity, the desire, and the ability to seek and assimilate new information. Four years at Wellesley can provide the foundation for the widest possible range of ambitions and the necessary self-confidence to fulfill them. At Wellesley, a student has every educational opportunity. Above all, it is Wellesley's purpose to teach students to apply knowledge wisely and to use the advantages of talent and education to seek new ways to serve the wider community."

Wesleyan University

The Stewart M. Reid House, 70 Wyllys Avenue, Middletown, CT 06459-0265

Academics

"You live with the coolest people in the world, which is interrupted periodically by instruction from the smartest people on campus," says a sophomore about a Wesleyan education. "There is a serious but noncompetitive academic environment,"

Selectivity Rating	97
Undergraduate Enrollment	2,722
Average SAT Verbal	680
Middle 50% SAT Verbal	640–730
Average SAT Math	678
Middle 50% SAT Math	640–720
Average ACT	29
% Graduating in Top 10% of Class	68

reports a senior art history major. A junior government major says, "When your government professor is on a first-name basis with the White House and is an excellent teacher [to boot], you can't ask for better academics." A senior chemistry major proclaims, "Our hippie, flower-child reputation overshadows the fact that we have a great science department with opportunities you can't get anywhere else." A sophomore writes, "Professors really care about your opinions, and you're treated as an intellectual equal." Still, one junior dance major laments that "diversity university does not have a diverse faculty." Students enjoy their academic freedom. "Wesleyan's academic requirements give you tremendous freedom to design your own curriculum and to take classes you really want to be in." Learning takes place both in and out of class. Writes a sophomore, "I feel like much of my academic experience occurs outside of class because there is so much political activity and passionate discussion about campus and global issues." While the professors are universally admired, the administration "isn't really in touch with the students' wants and needs. They're like 'independent Ivy,' and we're like 'Can we smoke it?'" A senior neuroscience major adds, "The administration appears to be trying to make us like the schools I didn't want to go to." The registrar's office is the focus of displeasure. The online registration system might be revolutionary, but "online registration is hell; you're basically racing with all the people on the computers next to you," one junior writes.

Admissions Phone: 860-685-3000 • Fax: 860-685-3001 •
Financial Aid Phone: 860-685-2800 • E-Mail: admissions@wesleyan.edu •
Website: www.wesleyan.edu

The Inside Word

Wesleyan stacks up well against its very formidable competitors academically, yet due to these same competitors the university admits at a fairly high rate for an institution of its high caliber. Candidate evaluation is nonetheless rigorous. If you aren't one of the best students in your graduating class, it isn't likely that you will be very competitive in Wesleyan's applicant pool. Strong communicators can help open the doors by submitting persuasive essays and interviews that clearly demonstrate an effective match with the university.

FROM THE ADMISSIONS OFFICE

"Wesleyan's faculty recently adopted an innovative plan for curricular renewal that reaffirms the individual freedom and flexibility for which Wesleyan is so well known, but also signals a new direction for liberal arts education. The focus of the changes is to help students achieve a coherent education. Wesleyan's Dean of Admission and Financial Aid, Barbara-Ann Wilson, describes the qualities Wesleyan seeks in its students: 'In an admission process as individualized and personalized as Wesleyan's, we evaluate each candidate on academic strength, intellectual curiosity, commitment (or passion!), personal qualitites, and extracurricular talent.'"

Williams College

988 Main Street, Williamstown, MA 01267

Academics

Williams is "definitely a tough school." The courses are "very difficult," and the "academic rigor" is pretty stressful. Students must complete a variety of distribution requirements and attend winter session, a month-long term during

Selectivity Rating	98
Undergraduate Enrollment	2,020
Average SAT Verbal	701
Middle 50% SAT Verbal	660–760
Average SAT Math	694
Middle 50% SAT Math	650–750
Average ACT	30

which students pursue individualized and less traditional areas of academic interest. "I never thought that college would be so much work," says an exasperated first-year student. Still, Williams students are some of the most satisfied in the nation, and the "world-class" and "always accessible" faculty is the overwhelming reason why. They are "eager to teach" and "passionate" about their subjects. Williams professors are also entertaining. "I timidly walked into organic chemistry on the first day of class having heard nightmare stories from my friends at other schools," fondly recalls a junior. "My prof is standing in his underwear and his robe, pretending he is just starting his day. The point is to show that organic chemistry is all around us, from the moment we wake up. Okay, so maybe throwing raw eggs at us was a little much, but I definitely appreciated the attempt at humor." And Williams' "personable" profs are "genuinely concerned about the students' wellness." The administration at Williams is "very accessible as well." To top everything off, "the alumni are well connected and quite helpful to current students."

Admissions Phone: 413-597-2211 • Fax: 413-597-4052 •
Financial Aid Phone: 413-597-4181 • E-Mail: admissions@williams.edu •
Website: www.williams.edu

The Inside Word

As is typical of highly selective colleges, at Williams high grades and test
scores work more as qualifiers than to determine admissibility. Beyond a
strong record of achievement, evidence of intellectual curiosity, noteworthy
nonacademic talents, and a noncollege family background are some aspects
of a candidate's application that might make for an offer of admission. But
there are no guarantees—the evaluation process here is rigorous. The
admissions committee (the entire admissions staff) discusses each candidate
in comparison to the entire applicant pool. The pool is divided alphabetically
for individual reading; after weak candidates are eliminated, those who remain
undergo additional evaluations by different members of the staff. Admission
decisions must be confirmed by the agreement of a plurality of the committee.
Such close scrutiny demands a well-prepared candidate and application.

FROM THE ADMISSIONS OFFICE

"Special course offerings at Williams include Oxford-style tutorials, where
students research and defend ideas, engaging in weekly debate with a peer
and a faculty tutor. Annually 30 Williams students devote a full year to the
tutorial method of study at Oxford; a quarter of Williams students pursue
their education overseas. Four weeks of Winter Study each January provide
time for individualized projects, research, and novel fields of study. Students
compete in 28 Division III athletic teams, perform in 25 musical groups, stage
10 theatrical productions, and volunteer in 30 service organizations. The
college receives several million dollars annually for undergraduate science
research and equipment. The town offers two distinguished art museums,
and 2,200 forest acres—complete with a treetop canopy walkway—for
environmental research and recreation."

Yale University

PO Box 208234, New Haven, CT 06520-8234

Academics

Yale "is truly one of America's great schools," writes one college counselor. It's an assertion that's hard to debate. As a major national research

Selectivity Rating	99
Undergraduate Enrollment	5,351
Middle 50% SAT Verbal	690–780
Middle 50% SAT Math	690–770
% Graduating in Top 10% of Class	95

center, Yale attracts many of the world's great scholars. But unlike other research institutes, Yale also devotes a lot of attention to undergraduates. Reports one student, "There is a genuine focus on undergraduates here. The professors seem genuinely to enjoy teaching, and you really do learn a lot in classes." Students do complain, however, that too many classes at all levels are taught by TAs and that they occasionally encounter professors who are poor teachers. Strife on campus over TAs' demands for higher wages and union representation has also been a cause of concern, heated debate, high anxiety, and student anger at the administration. Indeed, survey respondents consistently cited the administration as the worst aspect of the Yale undergrad experience. As one student puts it, "The administration does its absolute best to squelch student input." Academic departments are "uniformly excellent" here; among the school's many fine departments, standouts include drama, English, history, and the pre-med program. Yale has no core curriculum, instead requiring students to complete a broad range of general education requirements. Students tell us they like the "shopping period" registration system; they don't formally register for classes until two weeks into the semester, so the likelihood of getting stuck with a lousy class is minimized.

Admissions Phone: 203-432-9300 • Fax: 203-432-9392 •
Financial Aid Phone: 203-432-0360 • E-Mail: undergraduate.admissions@yale.edu •
Website: www.yale.edu

The Inside Word

Yale posted some impressive numbers for the class of 2000, the largest class in 10 years and a result of the highest yield in 25 years of admits who enrolled. After such a fabulous year it was inevitable that apps would drop a bit, and they have. Still, Yale is ultra-selective. And there's nothing to be gained by appealing a denial here—the admissions committee considers virtually all of its decisions final. Yale uses a regional review process that serves as a preliminary screening for all candidates, and only the best-qualified, well-matched candidates actually come before the admissions committee.

FROM THE ADMISSIONS OFFICE

"The most important questions the admissions committee must resolve are 'Who is likely to make the most of Yale's resources?' and 'Who will contribute significantly to the Yale community?' These questions suggest an approach to evaluating applicants that is more complex than whether Yale would rather admit well-rounded people or those with specialized talents. In selecting a class of 1,300 from approximately 15,000 applicants, the admissions committee looks for academic ability and achievement combined with such personal characteristics as motivation, curiosity, energy, and leadership ability. The nature of these qualities is such that there is no simple profile of grades, scores, interests, and activities that will assure admission. Diversity within the student population is important, and the admissions committee selects a class of able and contributing individuals from a variety of backgrounds and with a broad range of interests and skills."

Appendix III

Comparative Lists

The following lists are provided for you to see how the thirty-two schools in this book stack up against each other in a variety of measures. The lists should be read from top to bottom for increasing to decreasing competitiveness.

School	Acceptance Rate
United States Coast Guard Academy	9
Harvard College	11
Princeton University	12
United States Military Academy	13
Cooper Union	13
Stanford University	13
California Institute of Technology	13
Columbia University	14
United States Naval Academy	15
Massachusetts Institute of Technology	16
Yale University	16
Brown University	16
United States Air Force Academy	18
Amherst College	19
Dartmouth College	21
Georgetown University	22
University of Pennsylvania	23
Rice University	23
Williams College	24
Swarthmore College	24
Middlebury College	25
Duke University	26
Wesleyan University	27
Bates College	29
Cornell University	31

Haverford College	32
Johns Hopkins University	32
Northwestern University	33
University of Notre Dame	34
Washington and Lee University	35
Davidson College	36
Wellesley College	43

The acceptance rate is the total number of admitted students to the freshman class divided by the total number of applications for freshman admission each school received.

School	Freshman Retention Rate
Middlebury College	99
Massachusetts Institute of Technology	98
Yale University	98
Princeton University	98
Amherst College	98
Stanford University	98
California Institute of Technology	98
University of Notre Dame	97
Duke University	97
University of Pennsylvania	97
Columbia University	97
Swarthmore College	97
Harvard College	96
Williams College	96
Georgetown University	96
Dartmouth College	96
Brown University	96
Wesleyan University	96
Johns Hopkins University	96
Cornell University	96
Wellesley College	96
Rice University	96
United States Naval Academy	95
Northwestern University	95
Davidson College	95

Bates College	94
Haverford College	94
Washington and Lee University	94
United States Military Academy	92
Cooper Union	92
United States Air Force Academy	88
United States Coast Guard Academy	83

The freshman retention rate is the number of students who return for their sophomore year divided by the number of students who enrolled as freshman the previous year.

School	Number Applied
Cornell University	20,199
University of Pennsylvania	18,823
Stanford University	18,363
Harvard College	18,161
Brown University	16,806
Northwestern University	14,725
Georgetown University	14,237
Duke University	13,986
Princeton University	13,654
Columbia University	13,013
Yale University	12,887
United States Military Academy	11,473
Massachusetts Institute of Technology	10,671
United States Naval Academy	10,296
Dartmouth College	10,188
University of Notre Dame	10,051
United States Air Force Academy	9,548
Johns Hopkins University	9,445
Wesleyan University	6,862
Rice University	6,802
United States Coast Guard Academy	5,557
Amherst College	5,352
Middlebury College	5,154
Williams College	4,955
Bates College	4,240

Swarthmore College	3,956
California Institute of Technology	3,515
Davidson College	3,142
Washington and Lee University	3,057
Wellesley College	3,025
Haverford College	2,683
Cooper Union	2,216

Number of applications received by the admissions offices for the class of 2005.

School	SAT Verbal	SAT Math
Harvard College	700-800	700-790
Yale University	690-780	690-770
Duke University	640-740	660-760
Rice University	650-750	660-760
Williams College	660-760	650-750
Amherst College	650-760	650-740
Georgetown University	640-720	640-730
Washington and Lee University	630-720	640-710
Haverford College	630-730	630-720
Bates College	620-710	630-700
California Institute of Technology	727	776
Massachusetts Institute of Technology	709	757
Princeton University	740	750
Stanford University	715	717
Dartmouth College	708	713
Johns Hopkins University	670	711
University of Pennsylvania	683	709
Swarthmore College	718	706
Cooper Union	680	700
Cornell University	660	700
Middlebury College	710	700
Northwestern University	676	699
Columbia University	701	693
Brown University	690	690
University of Notre Dame	660	681
Wesleyan University	680	678

Wellesley College	684	669
United States Naval Academy	637	667
Davidson College	659	663
United States Air Force Academy	625	652
United States Military Academy	627	641
United States Coast Guard Academy	612	639

The colleges at the top of this list reported only the *range* of their SAT scores rather than the average. The range is what applicants in the 25th and 75th percentiles of admitted students scored.

School	Transfer Applications Received (Accepted)
United States Military Academy	0 (0)
United States Naval Academy	0 (0)
United States Air Force Academy	0 (0)
Princeton University	0 (0)
United States Coast Guard Academy	0 (0)
Haverford College	84 (3)
Yale University	751 (36)
Amherst College	183 (10)
Harvard College	1,153 (73)
Cooper Union	691 (46)
Columbia University	949 (63)
Duke University	303 (23)
Stanford University	1,217 (113)
Middlebury College	267 (27)
Bates College	145 (17)
Williams College	80 (10)
Johns Hopkins University	399 (54)
Massachusetts Institute of Technology	290 (43)
California Institute of Technology	151 (22)
Swarthmore College	117 (17)
Rice University	530 (78)
Washington and Lee University	64 (13)
Dartmouth College	235 (55)
University of Pennsylvania	1,583 (380)
Wellesley College	103 (27)

Wesleyan University	415 (118)
Northwestern University	529 (166)
Brown University	688 (200)
Georgetown University	1,313 (424)
Cornell University	1,976 (754)
Davidson College	34 (17)
University of Notre Dame	400 (210)

Transfer applicants must be enrolled as students at an institute of higher learning prior to their application for admission to another college.

School	Tuition
United States Military Academy	$0
United States Naval Academy	$0
United States Air Force Academy	$0
United States Coast Guard Academy	$0
Cooper Union	$8,300
Rice University	$16,600
Washington and Lee University	$19,170
California Institute of Technology	$20,904
University of Pennsylvania	$22,682
Harvard College	$22,694
Davidson College	$22,873
Wellesley College	$23,718
Georgetown University	$23,952
Columbia University	$24,150
University of Notre Dame	$24,320
Stanford University	$24,441
Williams College	$24,619
Cornell University	$24,760
Swarthmore College	$24,950
Yale University	$25,220
Wesleyan University	$25,380
Amherst College	$25,600
Brown University	$25,600
Haverford College	$25,826
Northwestern University	$25,839

Duke University	$26,000
Princeton University	$26,160
Johns Hopkins University	$26,220
Dartmouth College	$26,400
Massachusetts Institute of Technology	$26,960
Bates College	*$32,650 - Comprehensive
Middlebury College	*$32,765 - Comprehensive

Since all of these colleges, with the exception of the academies, which don't charge tuition, are private, the amount listed is the tuition for any student, regardless of state residency.

*Comprehensive tuition refers to the amount of tuition and room and board combined.

School	Yield %
United States Air Force Academy	91
United States Naval Academy	81
Harvard College	79
United States Military Academy	74
Princeton University	68
Stanford University	66
United States Coast Guard Academy	66
Yale University	65
Cooper Union	64
University of Notre Dame	57
Massachusetts Institute of Technology	56
University of Pennsylvania	56
Columbia University	55
Brown University	53
Dartmouth College	50
Cornell University	49
Georgetown University	48
Williams College	45
Wellesley College	45
Duke University	43
California Institute of Technology	43
Middlebury College	43
Amherst College	42
Washington and Lee University	42
Davidson College	41

Rice University	40
Northwestern University	39
Haverford College	39
Swarthmore College	39
Bates College	38
Wesleyan University	38
Johns Hopkins University	33

Yield is the percentage of accepted applicants for freshman admission who enroll at the college.

Appendix IV

College Process Resources

There is a world of information about the college process that is readily available to high schoolers and parents. The following listing of resources may prove to be helpful. The more you know about what to expect, the more successful your application process will be.

Getting In by Bill Paul (Addison-Wesley, 1995). This book may be the best inside look ever written about elite admissions. Princeton alum Bill Paul spent an entire admissions season observing the Princeton admissions process from inside the admissions committee. He follows the ups and downs of a group of applicants as they pursue Princeton and other top colleges. If you're hungry for a picture about what it's really like inside the Ivy League admissions process, this is the book for you.

A Is for Admission by Michele Hernandez (Warner Books, 1997). This book caused quite a stir when it came out. Michele Hernandez, former Dartmouth College admissions associate, reveals some previously unexamined Ivy League secrets, mainly the mysterious Academic Index. You find a lot of quantitative information as well as perspectives on how Dartmouth views various aspects of the application process.

The Best 331 Colleges by The Princeton Review (Random House, 2001). This perennial bestseller compiles data taken from thousands of student surveys from across the country. There are also interesting subjective ratings of quality of life, academics, admissions difficulty, and financial aid. Also included are inside perspectives on admissions criteria, deadlines, and Web addresses. In all, *The Best 331* is a highly accessible compendium of pertinent college data. The authoritative and good-humored approach makes it all the more enjoyable.

Review.com is the most heavily trafficked college resource on the Web. Review.com is far more than just an undergraduate college information site. It also covers such areas as careers and professional and graduate schools. There are all kinds of helpful essays on everything from college interviews to SAT strategies. You can read about the many Princeton Review books—like this one—and select from the wide range of test-preparation titles. One especially busy area is the discussion-forum group, which covers college issues, parent perspectives, law school, medical school, business school, careers, and more.

On Writing the College Application Essay by Harry Bauld (Barnes & Noble Books, 1987). This is the best essay book yet written. It's just a small-format, 138-page paperback that can be read in one evening, but its effect can be most powerful. Harry Bauld is a former Ivy League admissions officer who can write with a sense of humor and clear purpose. Once you understand your "place in the pile," you'll come to understand the strategic importance of the essay as a tool to pry open the elite-college gates. Even though the book is fifteen years old, its message is as pertinent as ever, especially in light of the tremendous increases in Ivy applications over the past decade.

The Elements of Style by Will Strunk and E.B. White (Allyn and Bacon, 1979). This is another classic on how to write well. Although not targeted specifically at college essays, the wisdom in its less-than-100 pages could fill a writer's library. The authors waste not one word in covering just about every crucial rule of grammar, usage, and style. If you can afford only one book on writing, this should be the one.

Cracking the SAT by The Princeton Review (Random House, 2001). This is the all-time classic self-help SAT-prep book. If you want to raise your score but don't have the time, money, or motivation for a formal coaching course, this is the next-best thing. The real appeal of this book is its readability and good sense of humor. It will also demystify the SAT as a test and as a process, revealing it for what it is—just another hurdle on your way to attending a great college.

Cracking the SAT IIs by The Princeton Review (Random House, 2001). Most top colleges require three knowledge-based ETS Subject Tests (Math, Writing, and a third of your choice). As with the SAT I the best way to prepare for these, other than paying attention in class, is to become familiar with the tests' format and content. The Princeton Review covers them all. There is also a related line of Princeton Review books addressing Advanced Placement exams.

The Princeton Review's How to Pay for College Without Going Broke (Random House, 2001). Author Kalman Chany is a nationally recognized expert on financial aid. He has poured his wisdom into this comprehensive guide for students and parents. The federal and institutional financial aid methodologies can seem completely incomprehensible to most families. Chany walks readers through a step-by-step explanation of filling out the two major financial aid forms, the FAFSA and the CSS Profile. As with prepping for the SATs, the biggest help when applying for financial aid is knowing what to expect when it comes time to do it. You'll feel like something of an expert after reading Chany's explanations. He also addresses common special circumstances such as custodial-parent responsibilities, student equity holdings, and assessment percentages.

Please Understand Me II by David Keirsey and Marilyn Bates (Prometheus Books, 1998). From the publisher: "Keirsey and Bates's *Please Understand Me*, first published in 1978, sold nearly 2 million copies in its first twenty years, becoming a perennial bestseller all over the world. Perhaps it was the user-friendly way that *Please Understand Me* helped people find their personality styles. Perhaps it was the simple accuracy of Keirsey's portraits of temperament and character types. Or perhaps it was the book's essential message—that members of families and institutions are okay even though they are fundamentally different from each other, and that they would all do well to appreciate their differences and give up trying to change others into copies of themselves." This book is an indispensable companion to Chapter 5.

CollegeBoard.org is the official site of The College Board, the publisher of the SAT. From this platform, you'll be able to find out all about the various tests that await you during your college quest: the SAT I, SAT II, AP exams, and more. There is also a wide selection of other college admissions information that you may find interesting.

The Chronicle of Higher Education is not just for higher education professionals. This weekly, multipart, tabloid-style newspaper is the best source of news and information about the latest happenings on the college front. *The Chronicle's* Web site, www.chronicle.com, is also a rich reserve of articles, job listings, and daily news headlines. The search engine is one of the best out there, and even non-subscribers can take advantage of the site's content.

Glossary

There are many specialized terms associated with college admissions. This list of definitions is hardly exhaustive but will provide you with some basic explanations. For more information on any one of these, search for it on the Web via your favorite search engine.

Adcom: Short for admissions committee.

Application Packaging: The art of creating an appealing and revealing physical application package, including the look and extent of the information contained therein. This is especially crucial when applying to exceedingly competitive colleges such as those in the Ivy League and others with acceptance rates in the well-under-50% realm. Although there is a small trend by selective colleges to accept—and even prefer—the Common Application, applicants must remember that the Common Application, even with its school-specific supplements, does not prompt for information that can be of great help in showing the admissions committee more about the applicant. See Chapter 7 for specifics on what to include.

Behavioral Preferences: Those natural preferences that, once identified, can offer insight into an individual's personality and temperament and provide a relatively accurate prediction of behavior. According to Myers-Briggs personality theory and the temperament postulates of David Keirsey, these preferences represent the individual's natural gravitation toward one or the other of two extremes on four dynamic behavioral poles: introversion and extraversion, sensing and intuiting, thinking and feeling, and perceiving and judging. See Chapter 5 and www.keirsey.com for complete details.

Common Application: A standardized, Web-based college application format accepted by many colleges. Using the Common Application has certain time advantages by allowing the applicant to apply to multiple colleges without having to re-enter basic application information. Many colleges have a college-specific supplement for the Common Application that adds information and writing requirements. See www.commonapp.org for more information.

CSS Financial Aid Profile: A financial aid application form and process administered by the College Scholarship Service. Most private colleges and universities require the CSS Profile. Unlike the FAFSA, an application fee is required. A FAFSA must always be filed in order to be considered for financial aid, regardless of whether or not a CSS Profile is required.

Deferral: A disappointing outcome of Early Decision or Early Action applications in which the acceptance decision on the applicant is not made early, but deferred to be made with all Regular Decision applicants in the spring. Deferral does not mean rejection, and in many cases merely delays acceptance from December–January until March–April.

EA: See *Early Action*.

Early Action: A type of early application process whereby the applicant submits his or her application usually by early November and receives notification of acceptance, deferral, or rejection by mid-December. Early Action (EA) applications are nonbinding. That is, applicants may choose to accept or reject a college's EA acceptance. Applicants usually have until May 1 to advise colleges of their enrollment decisions. There are several versions of EA plans, known mainly as EA 1, EA 2, EA I (or II), etc. Multiple EA programs allow applicants to apply beyond the usual early-November regular-EA deadline, but still receive a decision before the college's standard Regular Decision (RD) response date. In many cases, applicants may apply EA to more than one college. However, if the applicant has applied Early Decision, she usually may not apply to other colleges EA, although there may be exceptions to this rule. Always check your candidate college's application instructions and/or Web site for the specific EA/ED policies that apply.

Early Decision: A type of early application process whereby the applicant submits his application, usually by early November, and receives notification of acceptance, deferral, or rejection by mid-December. Unlike EA programs, however, the Early Decision (ED) process is binding. That is, the applicant signs a document pledging to enroll if the college to which he is applying accepts him early. If the applicant is deferred to the *Regular Decision* applicant pool, then the pledge to enroll is nullified. Usually, if an applicant applies under ED, the ED college will prohibit the applicant from applying early elsewhere, although there may be exceptions to this rule. Always check your candidate college's application instructions and/ or Web site for the specific ED policies that apply. Certain colleges may have multiple ED programs available that offer applicants more than one ED deadline, but function under the same binding-enrollment policy.

ECs: Short for extracurricular activities, or extracurriculars. Extracurriculars include a high schooler's activities that fall beyond the scope of purely academic (classroom) endeavors. Examples include sports, clubs, volunteer work, community service, jobs, personal hobbies, and so forth. The quality and depth of extracurriculars are a crucial part of elite college applications.

ED: See *Early Decision*.

EFC: Short for Expected Family Contribution. This is the amount a family is expected to contribute toward its child's college costs. The EFC is calculated (for public schools) according to the federal government's methodology (via the FAFSA) and/or (for private colleges) by an institutional (college-specific) methodology (via the CSS Profile and, possibly, the college's own financial aid form). The EFC amount is the difference between the college's total annual student budget (tuition, room and board, and any ancillary costs) and any school-provided financial aid (grants, loans, scholarships, work study, etc.).

Elite College: An imprecise, colloquial term used most often to refer to America's most selective colleges and universities. Many times, elite refers to those national colleges and universities appearing in the top 25 positions of the annual (and controversial) *U.S. News Best Colleges* rankings. Some observers may consider a college or university that accepts considerably less than half its applicants to be elite.

FAFSA: Short for Free Application for Federal Student Aid. This form is the main vehicle for students and families to obtain college financial aid. There is no application fee required to submit an FAFSA form. See www.fafsa.org for more information.

Individualized Study: A method for undergraduates to tailor a college's course offerings to their own general preferences. Other names for this approach include open curriculum, non-core curriculum, program of emphasis (POE), certificate program, and dual degree. Brown University is famous for its lack of core curriculum and the freedom its undergraduates have in shaping a truly self-designed degree program. Princeton University's certificate program allows students to declare one specific major, such as electrical engineering, and then obtain a certificate in a seemingly unrelated area, such as international studies. These flexible curricula are becoming more and more popular because of the blurring of the lines between traditional workplace disciplines.

Ivy League: A sports league. The term, however, has become synonymous with the highest prestige in American higher education. The eight schools comprising the Ivy League are (in current 2000 *U.S. News*-ranking order): Princeton University,

Harvard University, Yale University, University of Pennsylvania, Dartmouth College, Columbia University, Cornell University, and Brown University. The term "Ivy" is also used colloquially to refer to some so-called elite colleges, although, technically, there are only eight Ivy League schools.

Liberal Arts: In general, the group of college courses and disciplines offering the widest possible approach to life knowledge. College liberal arts programs strive to educate students in basic disciplines of the humanities and the social and behavioral sciences and provide general-education courses that enrich cultural understanding. In many cases, a liberal arts major can propel a student to law, medical, or business school.

Merit-Based Aid: Financial aid (sometimes referred to as a scholarship) awarded by a college irrespective of a student's financial need. Merit awards are sometimes made as a result of high SAT scores, high class rank, high GPAs, or similar academic achievements. Merit aid is granted in addition to need-based aid and can significantly improve a financial-aid package. Merit awards can also come from getting a high score on the PSAT/NMSQT, resulting in the student becoming a National Merit Scholar. Some colleges and universities offer significant merit scholarships to students who become National Merit Semi-Finalists.

Need-Based Aid: Financial aid awarded according to a student's/family's financial need as assessed by various methodologies (see EFC). Several top colleges and universities offer to meet 100% of a student's/family's financial need. In general, financial aid packages from these schools provide aid that covers 100% of the difference between a family's EFC and the total annual student budget. The aid packages comprise grants, scholarships, loans, and work-study.

Perceived Value: The subjective opinion students, parents, and employers have about the relative educational quality offered by various colleges. Contrary to the popular Total Quality tenet, perception is not always reality. For example, it is entirely possible to get an education at the state university-level that can at least rival that of a so-called elite private university. However, the general perception among many students, parents, and employers is that the elite college graduate will have the superior education. Obviously, this is a generality and each case must be evaluated individually. Parents and students who are focused on the college degree as a means of obtaining a profitable life's work would do well to investigate the job placement data of any candidate college. Many lesser-known colleges have quite surprising placement success rates, contrary to their popular value perceptions.

Personal Statement: Another term for the application essay. Personal statements are one of the most crucial parts of elite college applications.

PSAT/NMSQT: Short for Preliminary Scholastic Assessment Test/ National Merit Scholarship Qualifying Test. Most often taken by high schoolers in October of the junior year, this slightly simplified version of the SAT I provides most students with an introduction to standardized tests administered by the Educational Testing Service (ETS). Scores from the PSAT also enter the student into competition for the nationwide National Merit Scholarship competition. The test has a verbal, math, and writing component.

Quality Applicant: A college applicant who not only meets, but in many cases exceeds the profile criteria of recently admitted applicants to a particular college. The case for quality extends beyond sheer numbers, though, and into the realm of writing skills (for the essay), application packaging, quality recommendations, and—to a lesser extent—interview skills.When the match between a student and a college is strong across the board, the candidate can be considered to be one of quality.

Recs: Short for recommendations. Applicants to highly selective colleges and universities are usually required to submit two teacher recs along with their counselor's rec. Many applicants also submit one or two additional recs from people who know them well and can speak compellingly about the applicant's personal qualities.

Regional Representative:The person in a college's admission office who has responsibility for applicants from a particular geographical area.When applicants need to communicate with admissions, the regional representative is usually the best person to contact.

Regular Decision: The application option attracting the largest number of college applicants. At elite colleges, Regular Decision (RD) applications are usually due January 1–15 and admission decisions are usually rendered from mid-March through early April. Unlike Early Decision, RD is not binding. Accepted RD applicants are not obligated to enroll.

Sanitized Information: In reference to the annual *U.S. News* college rankings, it is one of their procedures that can offer a misleading picture of a college's year-to-year precise quantitative data. For example, a college has three consecutive years of 30% alumni participation in annual giving, and then, in the fourth year (due to a concentrated developmental effort), experiences a surge to 45% participation. *U.S. News* will, for the purposes of its forthcoming rankings, take a three-year average, absorbing the most recent year's 50% increase in alumni giving, and smooth (or "sanitize") the giving data, thus obscuring the marked increase and its implications. Since different colleges report different data to various agencies, foundations, surveys, etc., *U.S. News* must necessarily find a way to standardize responses so that colleges don't excessively inflate their survey answers. However, the results of the surveys can therefore be fuzzy.

SAR: Short for Student Aid Report. This is the form all FAFSA filers receive after they fill out their FAFSA information. Generally, it merely verifies the information that is submitted, but in some cases the filer may have to update some information or correct something that has been mistakenly input. It is very important to be certain that the information on the SAR is correct because your financial aid award (if you qualify for aid) will be based on this information.

Short Response: A relatively brief written response prompted by a question on the college application. Many elite-college applications have three to six (or more) of these short response questions. They require careful consideration and should not be dismissed with a lackluster effort because of their seeming brevity.

Student Profile Marketing: The systematic process that applicants should use to present themselves in the best and fullest light to admissions committees. Some aspects of profile marketing include knowing how to reveal the greatest possible amount of personal information in specific application responses, selecting the right kinds of materials to augment written responses, understanding the importance of follow-up and regular communication with the admissions representative, and other tactics and strategies.

Study Abroad and International Programs: Specific curriculum options that offer undergraduates the chance to leave the United States for a semester or year of study at colleges overseas. Traditional study-abroad programs involve students in their junior years, once they have declared particular programs of concentration. Colleges develop close ties with foreign colleges and universities and exchange students on a regular basis. Many colleges offer international programs that offer not only traditional courses tailored to those majors, but also the option to spend one or two semesters of foreign study in the context of an international study-abroad program. Although students in these majors are encouraged to go abroad, study abroad is not required.

Top-25: See *Elite College*.

Waitlist: A kind of admissions twilight zone reserved for applicants who are neither accepted nor rejected. Applicants are assigned to the waitlist when final acceptance and rejection letters go out. Although students gain admission to top colleges from waitlists every year, it can be a very agonizing process with no promises of admission. As a general rule, waitlisted applicants at more highly selective colleges have a relatively lower chance of gaining acceptance than waitlisted applicants at less selective colleges.

About the Authors

Dave Berry has been helping students get into the best colleges for well over a decade. Specializing in Ivy League and Top-25 admissions, Dave is an expert in the areas of student stats evaluation, college matching, application essays, personality and temperament assessment, and Web-based college counseling. He also moderates The Princeton Review's parents-only discussion forum on the popular Review.com Web site. His syndicated Q&A column, *College Knowledge*, won the Newspaper Association of America Foundation's 1997 Program Excellence Award and his cable television series of the same name airs in 85,000 central-Pennsylvania homes. Dave resides in Altoona, Pennsylvania.

David Hawsey is vice president for enrollment at Albion College in Michigan. Over the last two decades, he has served as a higher education administrator, guest speaker, consultant, and adjunct faculty member. He has held positions of director, dean, associate vice president, and vice president in Carnegie-classified Baccalaureate colleges, Masters, Doctoral I and Research I universities nationwide. In addition to Albion College, David has served Drexel University, Penn State University, Pacific Lutheran University, and Juniata College. His responsibilities have included strategic planning and management in alumni relations, admissions, development, financial aid, and marketing. He also consults with private colleges and universities to develop integrated marketing plans for enrollment management, alumni relations, and fundraising. Additional positions in for-profit corporate communications, public relations, and information systems development have helped him to identify what both colleges and high school students should have in their marketing toolboxes. His unique insider perspective gives colleges, prospective students, and their families a crucial advantage during the challenging college-search process.

Notes

Notes

Notes

Notes

Notes

Notes

Notes

Notes

Notes

Notes

Notes

Notes

FIND US...

International

Hong Kong
4/F Sun Hung Kai Centre
30 Harbour Road, Wan Chai,
Hong Kong
Tel: (011)85-2-517-3016

Japan
Fuji Building 40, 15-14
Sakuragaokacho, Shibuya Ku,
Tokyo 150, Japan
Tel: (011)81-3-3463-1343

Korea
Tae Young Bldg, 944-24,
Daechi- Dong, Kangnam-Ku
The Princeton Review- ANC
Seoul, Korea 135-280,
South Korea
Tel: (011)82-2-554-7763

Mexico City
PR Mex S De RL De Cv
Guanajuato 228 Col. Roma
06700 Mexico D.F., Mexico
Tel: 525-564-9468

Montreal
666 Sherbrooke St.
West, Suite 202
Montreal, QC H3A 1E7 Canada
Tel: 514-499-0870

Pakistan
1 Bawa Park - 90 Upper Mall
Lahore, Pakistan
Tel: (011)92-42-571-2315

Spain
Pza. Castilla, 3 - 5º A, 28046
Madrid, Spain
Tel: (011)341-323-4212

Taiwan
155 Chung Hsiao East Road
Section 4 - 4th Floor,
Taipei R.O.C., Taiwan
Tel: (011)886-2-751-1243

Thailand
Building One, 99 Wireless Road
Bangkok, Thailand 10330
Tel: 662-256-7080

Toronto
1240 Bay Street, Suite 300
Toronto M5R 2A7 Canada
Tel: 800-495 7737
Tel: 716-839 4391

Vancouver
4212 University Way NE,
Suite 204
Seattle, WA 98105
Tel: 206-548 1100

National (U.S.)

We have over 60 offices around the U.S. and
run courses in over 400 sites. For courses and locations
within the U.S. call 1-800- 2- Review and you will be
routed to the nearest office.

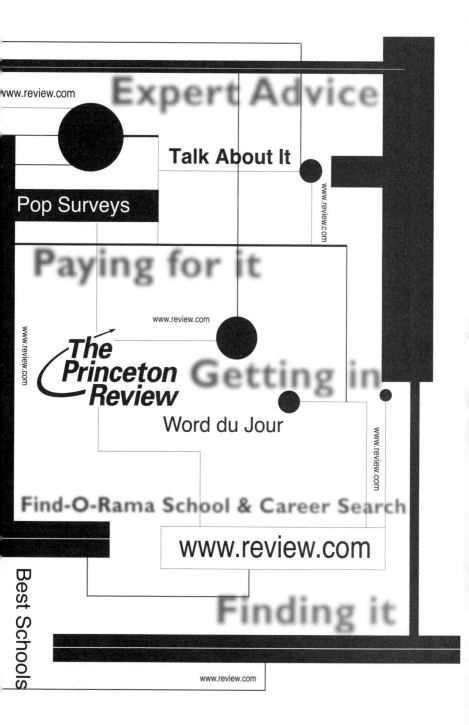

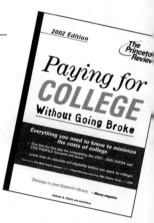